e-Commerce and the Law

The legal implications of doing business online

ANDREW SPARROW

FINANCIAL TIMES

Prentice Hall

An imprint of Pearson Education

London	New York	San Francisco	Toronto	Sydney
Tokyo	Singapore	Hong Kong	Cape Town	Madrid
Paris	Milan	Munich	Amsterdam	

PEARSON EDUCATION LIMITED

Head Office:
Edinburgh Gate
Harlow CM20 2JE
Tel: +44 (0)1279 623623
Fax: +44 (0)1279 431059

London Office:
128 Long Acre
London WC2E 9AN
Tel: +44 (0)20 7447 2000
Fax: +44 (0)20 7240 5771
Website: www.business-minds.com

First published in Great Britain in 2000

© Pearson Education Limited 2000

The right of Andrew Sparrow to be identified as author
of this work has been asserted by him in accordance
with the Copyright, Designs and Patents Act 1988.

ISBN 0 273 64565 X

British Library Cataloguing in Publication Data
A CIP catalogue record for this book can be obtained from the British Library.

10 9 8 7 6 5 4 3 2 1

Typeset by Boyd Elliott Typesetting
Printed and bound in Great Britain

The Publishers' policy is to use paper manufactured from sustainable forests.

e-Commerce and the Law

About the author

Andrew Sparrow LLB (Hons) is a national award-winning solicitor. A partner with Lee Crowder solicitors in Birmingham, Mr Sparrow is a specialist in corporate law and has a wide experience in commercial legal matters. He qualified as a solicitor of the Supreme Court in 1989 and an early interest in industry and commerce attracted him to commercial law. He spent the period following his qualification working at one of the country's leading national groups of legal firms.

Mr Sparrow is the author of the FT Prentice Hall book *The Responsibilities of Company Directors*, and also the author of two multimedia CD-Roms serving as client guides to the law. In addition, he wrote the script and planned the structure development of the official CD-Rom for the 1998 G8 Summit of World Leaders, winning *The Lawyer* national award for 'Best Use of Multimedia in the Law' for his CD-Roms in 1999. He has also written and appeared in over 16 television programmes aimed at training the legal profession in England and Wales. Mr Sparrow is also a regular contributor to a number of business magazines on commercial legal developments.

If you would like further details on any matter contained in this book, please contact Andrew Sparrow at:

Lee Crowder
Solicitors
39 Newhall Street
Birmingham
B3 3DY

Tel: 0121-236 4477
Fax: 0121-236 0774
E-mail: andrew.sparrow@leecrowder.co.uk

This book cannot be a substitute for specific advice and anyone contemplating important management decisions should take further advice.

Contents

Foreword

One of the central issues for all concerned with e-commerce is the regulatory framework which governs the internet. The law applies on-line as it does off-line – but the application of existing laws in a new medium is not always easy. It is, therefore, essential to help business people to understand the law of e-commerce, and to have confidence in the internet as a safe place to do business.

The internet, of course, is global. The more businesses understand the legal issues which relate to e-commerce, the more they can gain competitive advantage – whether their markets are global, local, or both.

I hope this book – pulling together both case law and statutes – will help directors and managers to trade on-line, and to succeed in this exciting and fast-changing business environment.

Patricia Hewitt MP
Minister for E-Commerce
Department of Trade and Industry

Table of cases

Table of statutes

Acknowledgements

The genesis of my interest in the law relating to e-commerce was in 1996. It seems hard to imagine given the complete familiarity with the medium now that as recently as four years ago very little was known about the Internet outside the IT community at large. It was curiosity which led me to attend a seminar in Birmingham given to explain what this rapidly emerging technology was. The invited audience was nothing if not sceptical of its significance to their businesses. I felt that if the medium was to be utilised for commercial trade then a legal framework around such activity would need to evolve so as to ensure that the World Wide Web is a safe environment in which to do business. I commenced a programme of research and found little or no published detail on the legal issues of trading on the Internet. That detail emerged piecemeal over the next few years.

Several seminars given to business audiences and articles in business journals followed, culminating in this book.

I wish to express my appreciation to Stephen Partridge, Acquisitions Editor, FT Prentice Hall for encouraging me to prepare this work. Any omissions, errors, inaccuracies or deficiencies are entirely my own responsibility.

I reserve the greatest thanks for my mother Muriel, sister Patricia and my brothers David, John and Paul, but especially to my darling wife, without whose unstinting support this book could not have been written.

Introduction

Max Freisch said of technology that it is 'the knack of arranging the world that we do not have to experience it.' This observation has particular application to a technology which itself operates in an electronic environment and has led to a new description to explain its character – the virtual world. The pace of development and the advance of technology is no longer measured in the span of decades but rather can be charted with the dawn of each year. It is evolution at the speed of revolution. The means of communication now open to government, commerce and society as a whole facilitates the instant global dissemination of information. So it is that one of those means of communication itself has assumed a level of growth at a rate unparalleled in the evolvement of communication systems. Perhaps only five years ago if one had posed the question to most individuals in this country, 'what is the Internet?' the response would not yield the answer which undoubtedly would be forthcoming today. It is impossible not to have heard of the Internet or the World Wide Web now. The speed at which this fascinating medium has entered common parlance is itself remarkable. This rapid development has been largely due to the development of the World Wide Web and the user-friendly 'browser' software which allows a user with scant knowledge of technology to connect to any website address in the world in seconds. While it took 38 years for broadcast radio to achieve 50 million users, it has taken the Internet a mere four. One prominent development is the convergence of existing technologies such as television, mobile phones and hand-held computers to incorporate Internet access.

It is nevertheless of more than passing note that in many ways the recent development of the Internet has not been fuelled by a headlong pursuit by the world of commerce to find a new, more effective means of conducting business. Thus, its metamorphosis from a military inspired concept, for years the preserve of North American universities, is at variance with the majority of innovations, be they of product or service, which are conceived with one aim in mind – their commercial potential. Yet a system which offers global access on a scale never before imagined has enormous commercial significance. It is this realisation which has seen the most dramatic increase in Internet use since its inception. Organisations from all fields of business and from all points in the modern world are turning their attention to how the World Wide Web might offer a sales and marketing potential hitherto unachievable. The Internet is not a stand-alone system, it is a great facilitator of information and commerce. It is also a disruptive technology. Many established businesses will be undermined by start-ups using new technologies. For the mature companies, the temptation not to embrace the

World Wide Web is based on apparent sound economics. Usually, newcomers tackle small or non-existent markets, offer lower functionality, earn lower prices and smaller profit margins. Companies need to pursue e-commerce outside the mainstream business with a full mandate to attack the latter. If mainstream business dominates the organisation's thinking, it may not secure the new opportunities e-commerce presents. The fact that companies are attuned to the significance of this technology to the business environment – albeit after a faltering start – must be welcomed. In many ways electronic commerce is not about technology. The technology is the enabling element of a strategy where the focus should remain an improved route to market and customer satisfaction. Issues such as customer fulfilment must be at the fore of any e-business planning.

However, with new technology comes new potential for dispute – on a scale difficult to comprehend and serving as a salutary warning to the use of the Internet. Thus with new methods of conducting business come new legal difficulties and uncertainties. The law in any enlightened society must always find a home and so it is that with the advent of electronic commerce necessarily must come regulation by the legal process. The global and anonymous nature of the Internet has created a demand for specific law. The law in the context of the Internet is not to be viewed as an unnecessary constraint upon the freedom of trade, but rather the only safeguard there exists to ensure the proper and fair dealing of business across all lands where opportunity exists.

Wealth and employment depend on knowing what your customers will buy and knowing how to pull together most effectively the people, commerce, equipment and all the materials needed to meet that customer need. Business survival and success depend on having the know-how to deliver this better than the competition. Knowledge as to how to secure the best advantage from the emerging communications technologies is increasingly crucial to all in that process. Electronic commerce is a key element of success for many UK businesses. It will rapidly become an essential in the success or failure of many more. It draws businesses, suppliers and customers closer together.

Electronic commerce has, however, caused existing laws, regulations and codes of practice to be left behind in the wake of this surge into online trading. As business in the United Kingdom embraces electronic commerce it must understand why the successful application of English law will afford the best chance of ensuring a sales environment which offers minimal risk and maximum potential. It is seen as delivering a long-held panacea for many companies and gives customers direct access to the company's products from their own premises. This book has been written to assist with the unravelling of these legal issues. There is a widely held belief among non-lawyers that the law never changes. This is not correct. The law is constantly changing, and the pace at which it changes is likely to quicken in the near future. The law is the mechanism by which the Internet will be organised, procedures managed, disputes resolved, and fairness and equity achieved.

It is also often said that the law has a language only understood by other lawyers. The IT world has similarly developed its own vernacular and the Internet has originated its own linguistic geography. Such private language is necessary for the comprehension of sometimes complex principles which are the preserve of each discipline. In this work, I have attempted to avoid unnecessary use of such language and articulate each issue in a style readily understood by the non-legal, and non-IT, layperson. The academic integrity of the matter reviewed is nonetheless sound.

This book is intended to help companies and managers control the impact of e-business. Over 180 questions are asked and answered.

I suggest that the best way to use this book is simply to read it through to the end, since in this way a general understanding of the overall scope of the law of electronic commerce will be obtained. You should then keep it for reference to the individual parts when the need arises. There are brief checklists of your broad responsibilities at the end of each chapter. The book is not a complete guide to English law on this subject. The object is to give the reader a broad outline and so provide guidance in the right direction.

The law is stated as at April 2000. However, the publishers are promoting a section of their website at http://www.business-minds.com in conjunction with this publication. This will facilitate the updating of the book from time to time by adding to the website consideration of significant developments. I hope this service will be a useful additional benefit to the reader.

The business potential of the Internet

Our doubts are traitors and make us lose the good we might win, by fearing to attempt.

Shakespeare, *Measure for Measure,* Act I, scene IV.

This book is written as a guide to the legal issues pertaining to an online business presence. The legal considerations are heavily associated with the business potential of the medium and it is therefore helpful to briefly examine the emerging commercial attraction of the Internet.

1.1 THE ATTRACTION OF THE INTERNET

Increased pressures on business urge companies to explore new channels. They include intense retail competition, industry maturity, falling margins, the need for differentiation and added value, and the desire for direct consumer contact – for manufacturers as well as retailers. It is inevitable that some products will sell better than others online or that they are more suited to this medium for a variety of reasons:

- *Delivery*. Items which are currently posted or are easy to post suit the Internet as does software, including games, which can be downloaded over the Internet itself. Bulky items, where home delivery is required in any event, may also suit the Internet.

- *Information-based selection and purchase*. The Internet is ideal for purchases which need collation and comparison such as PCs and insurance policies. It has improved the information on and display of goods already selling through catalogues, brochures or telesales.

- *Specialist or international items for which there is limited local access to the stock range.*

- *Chores or repeat purchases of goods.*

- *The demographics of the user*. Products suited to the precise profile of the typical web user today include PC products and leisure items.

Advantages of online sales include:

- lower distribution charges;

- larger audience and new profile of audience reached;

- ability to offer a wider range of stock;

- information capture about the consumer is facilitated and highly targeted micro-marketing is possible.

In many areas of commerce to be first into a new area is to invest most and waste most. However, this rationale does not hold true with the Internet. Not only are new business initiatives essential to attract investor interest or capital rating but early online presence is beneficial to obtain experience of the technology and of online marketing methods.

1.2 TAPPING THE POTENTIAL OF THE INTERNET

As the Internet matures as a business medium it will become clear which commercial applications work and which do not. The simple conversion of an offline sales process to an online environment may have commercial merits but will not of itself realise the medium's greatest potential. The e-commerce revolution which is oft referred to will be given full expression in the new business models which will develop by virtue of the medium. It is that potential for innovative change to business and services which represents the greatest opportunity for the modern commercial world.

It is business-to-business ('B2B') as opposed to business-to-consumer ('B2C') e-commerce which offers greatest potential for the Internet. If this is to be realised then increased speed or bandwidth and better information retrieval and search facilities will need to be developed. It is highly likely that current industry practices such as procurement, distribution, pricing, marketing, product development and customer service will be changed beyond recognition by the Internet.

What are the potential barriers to the growth of the Internet?

At the time of writing, there are a number of possible barriers to the development of the Internet as a commercial medium. Each of them has a legal dimension. Perceived risks include:

- the potential for virus attack, destructive e-mails and other security breaches;
- lack of a secure mechanism for transactions;
- the potential for users to access illegal or offensive material;
- problems with cultivating trust among customers;
- problems with implementing cross-border data protection;
- problems of avoiding defamation;
- problems of negotiating liability laws;
- inadequate or unclear regulation;
- problems of negotiating copyright and other intellectual property rights;
- problems of implementing cross-border taxation laws;

- inadequate brand protection;
- potential fraud by customers.

There is a view which is referred to as the productivity paradox. The paradox is simply this. While IT in general and the Internet in particular are increasingly widespread tools in industry, they appear to make no measurable contribution to economic growth. It should be understood that this observation only relates to the use of IT and the Internet, not the manufacture, supply or distribution of IT and Internet products and services.

How to set up your e-commerce business

2.1 INTRODUCTION

What is meant by electronic commerce?

Electronic commerce is simply about conducting business electronically. It is commerce based on the electronic processing and transmission of data, including text, sound and video. E-commerce entails the selling of your goods and services from your website over the Internet. This might include the online ordering and electronic delivery of material or supply of products. Alternatively it may be the provision of a service such as an advice line or an after-sales support line.

Electronic business, however, encapsulates many more processes. In commercial terms, a true e-business could be electronic almost from start to finish across the entire supply chain. While customers or other businesses place orders at a website, all the other functions – credit card authorisation, stock check, ledger update, delivery tracking, stock reorder and so on – happen seamlessly without any human intervention. Possibly, the only manual intervention is loading the goods at a warehouse and delivering them – and in the case of a service or electronic product such as digital music, there need be no human involvement at all.

However, for companies with limited information and technology expertise, the way forward in e-business can look far from straightforward. There is now a large array of suppliers purporting to offer everything from web-enabled switchboards to security tools for business 'extranets' to hosted solutions for almost every aspect of the business.

Business leaders are rapidly waking up to e-commerce reality. The threats it poses will not go away. Established companies are under pressure to seize early mover advantage, if only to protect their existing market positions. In this hothouse environment your company needs to strike the right balance between moving forward as quickly as it can and ensuring it is not running unnecessary risks.

This book is written to examine and explain the legal issues associated with the use of the Internet as a trading medium. However, for contextual purposes it is helpful to briefly consider some of the practical detail surrounding the establishment of your corporate sales website.

What is a website?

The World Wide Website which your organisation adopts is the most visible face of your company on the Internet. It amounts to a virtual shopfront or catalogue of your range of products or services for the benefit of potential or existing customers who will visit it. Your www site is simply a connection of separate pages the extent and complexity of which is determined by you. There are sites with thousands of pages and conversely some with only a few. Variation in complexity of those pages is demonstrated by the simple use of text and photographs in some instances, to sophisticated pages enabling customers to search for information, order products and pay for them online.

The technical basis of your website is the storage of text files that contain special formatting codes that describe how the text looks when displayed. These codes are part of a formatting language called hypertext mark-up language (HTML). This describes the size, colour and font style of your text and also any sound or video clips. The HTML codes are what enables visitors to your site to navigate from one page to another.

Whose hardware should my organisation use?

Many of the perceived dangers associated with using the Internet as a commercial medium relate to the way in which the underlying technology works, or its architecture. The key choice faced by your organisation when setting up an electronic commerce website is whether to set up a site yourself on your own hardware or to use another company, usually an Internet service provider (ISP) to host the service. This entails the ISP putting your website on a computer located at, and run by, the ISP. A major advantage of using an ISP is the saving made by your organisation by sharing the bandwidth connection to the Internet with the ISP's other customers. Against this must be balanced the risk of holding confidential company information on an external computer. This risk can, however, be curtailed by including carefully drafted contract terms in the agreement with your ISP.

2.2 DOMAIN NAMES

2.2.1 Domain name regulation

The Internet is increasingly used by commercial organisations to promote themselves and their products, and in some cases to buy and sell. In any business, the choice of name has a value far beyond its simple identification. The name your business adopts may well in time become instantly recognisable to your customers, suppliers and your business sector at large. It follows that when establishing an electronic business presence most will wish to replicate their established company name or devise a name which adequately establishes the nature of the business if it is one newly created, perhaps specifically for Internet trading. Thus, if your organisation is to pursue an electronic presence it will need to have an identity to enable visitors to find your website. In the world of electronic commerce that identity is accomplished by your domain name.

Domain names share a fundamental attribute with traditional trade marks (see section 7.4). Like trade marks, they serve as a public signalling device to identify and associate sites with particular sources of products and services. However, domain names also differ from trade marks because, whereas a trade mark has no utility beyond its information content, a domain name, like a telephone number or street number, has utility value as an address. Armed with your domain name, a potential customer can make contact and transact with your company.

The choice of your domain name should be the first issue you address when your company elects to establish a website. One of the most important steps in creating a web presence is to give your site an effective name. The name should be easy to remember and representative of your company. If your domain name is based on the name of the company or its key brands it will enable those who wish to access your site to locate it quickly. However, as the Internet has developed domain names have become a scarce resource. When more than one company attempts to obtain the same name dispute will arise. The availability of preferred domain names is hindered further by the constraints of the Internet medium itself.

Why should domain names have a value?

As trade marks and brands have become so important in marketing all types of products and services – not only at the consumer level, but also at the commercial and industrial levels – associated domain names have also become highly valuable assets in today's electronic environment. Domain names essentially exist in an electronic vacuum. As a consequence, some domain names have value to a broad range of commercial interests. Thus, registration and nurturing of domain names is critically important if you have a key brand or trade mark.

The very concept of valuing domain names or other digital assets, particularly ones linked to an established trade mark or brand, is increasingly a major issue. As domain names grow in importance to companies, the establishment of accurate domain names is increasingly necessary. Possession of the appropriate domain name in conjunction with the trade mark or brand will mean an increasing number of sales, trades and other transactions involving domain names. It is important to realise that the relatively small cost of registering a series of domain names does not compare to the hundreds of thousands of pounds of value that those same domain names might carry in the future.

What constraints add to the difficulties of domain name choice?

The clues which allow one to distinguish between two companies with similar names in the physical world do not exist on the Internet. An example might be the domain name *sun.co.uk*. It is unlikely that anyone would mistake the computer company for the newspaper of the same name in ordinary reference. However, both organisations could lay claim to this Internet address and the address alone does not make it possible to work out which company is using it.[1] The limitation of expression enforced by the domain name and which restricts availability is highlighted by another example which finds the domain name system at odds with the trade mark system (see section 7.4). In short, the same trade mark can be used for a number of different types of goods. A UK trade mark, for example 'Polo', can be registered to different companies under the trade mark system for confectionery, clothing and cars. However, for domain name purposes, this is not possible. Only one company can have the domain http://www.polo.co.uk/. Each domain name must therefore be unique.

The name of our limited company is registered at Companies House and thus cannot be registered by anyone else. Does that give us automatic protection of the name for Internet purposes?

No. If you are to enter the Internet environment for commercial reasons you need to register your domain name. This is an entirely distinct process from the legal requirement to register a company name and number. In the United Kingdom and indeed all over the world there exists a national registry of domain names. The registration procedure is in fact simple. It is possible for companies to register domain names themselves. Nonetheless, as a commercial entity it is prudent to use the services of a domain name agent. Such agents have established facilities to register the names in national registries across the globe. Indeed, as a matter of further precaution it is possible to register with more than one domain name agent. In doing so, your organisation will maximise the chance of adequately securing its chosen domain name.

If we are contemplating a domain name can we make a preliminary enquiry to establish its availability?

Yes. All domain registration agents have websites where you, as a potential purchaser, can instantly check at no cost to see if a particular domain name is still available. Indeed, registration is usually perfected over the Internet itself and therefore can be undertaken from anywhere in the world. The entire process can take as little as 15 seconds.

Your chosen domain name will be trailed by '.uk', for example, XYZ Limited.co.uk upon registration in the United Kingdom.

The wisdom of using a registration agent is heightened still further by the inevitable fact that in what is a global market there are necessarily differences between countries in terms of what is permissible for registration as a domain name. For example, the French national registry will not allow you to use a 'Fr' registration unless your organisation has offices in France and is registered for

VAT in that territory. A registration agent can provide you with detailed advice regarding national registration requirements and administrative problems.

Domain names are allocated by the various registrars on a first come, first served basis. So long as the name you request has not been chosen by another organisation, and subject to the trade mark issues discussed at section 7.4, registration is straightforward.

In this country who is responsible for maintaining the domain name registry?

It is a company called Nominet.uk. Nominet.uk is the naming authority for the UK. Its rules specify that it may cancel a registration, *inter alia*, because in Nominet.uk's opinion it is likely to cause confusion to Internet users. However, there are similar organisations in all developed countries. In the United States the function is discharged by InterNic which once again is a company specifically incorporated for this purpose. However, as national governmental regulations and cultures differ, each national registry has different policies for domain name registration.

It is clear that the choice of domain name registration agent is important. What are the questions we should consider when appointing an agent?

First, your organisation should ask whether the agent has ever been involved in litigation or disputes involving the name registry that you are interested in. Second, ask how many domain names the agents own themselves and do they ever register names to themselves to sell on to other people.

You should also consider the following questions:

- How will your organisation's name and the name of the agent appear on the registration card?
- Does the agent house names on their own server or have they contracted this task to someone else? If they use their own server, what back-up facilities do they supply?
- What guidance can they give on the dispute policy of the registration authority you are interested in?
- What is their policy concerning name conflict?

You should also check their terms and conditions and ask about the contract you will have with the registration authority. If you are seeking a 'co.uk' registration (see section 2.2.4 below), can they supply you with a set of Nominet.uk's terms and conditions? It is important for you to ask this because your organisation will be entering into a contract with the registration authority in addition to the registration agent.

2.2.2 Domain name categorisation

How are domain names categorised?

There are two forms of domain names. The first is *generic* and the second *country*.

Generic

The use of generic domains is in fact regulated not in the United Kingdom but by the United States National Standards Institute (NSI). It is important to appreciate the distinction here between choice and availability of your domain name which, as we have seen, is managed by Nominet.uk. The system is presently fairly relaxed and has historically favoured US organisations. This is because the United States remains the largest single user of the Internet and the growth of the World Wide Web has until recently been most apparent in North America. Examples of the free use of generic domains are the American colleges which use the global stem '.edu'. However, the relaxed application of generic domains also means that the '.com' domain which is usually applied to US companies is open to anyone.

What do generic domain names include?

The top-level generic domain names include:

- .com (commercial organisations);
- .net (network organisations);
- .org (miscellaneous organisations).

They are obtained from companies accredited by the Internet Corporation for Assigned Names and Numbers (ICANN).

Registration of a generic top-level domain name now lasts for ten years.

What is the advantage of using a .com suffix as opposed to a .uk registration?

There is no legal basis for the choice. If your organisation does intend to register domain names in other jurisdictions it might be useful to also secure a .com name in addition to your .co.uk registration.

In some instances, your business may wish to register a generic domain which has the attraction of not only including your chosen name but also makes clear the kind of business you are engaged in. Some firms of solicitors include the word 'law' within their domain name. Certainly, if your organisation has global ambitions, it should apply for a generic registration.

Country

Country domains are based upon an internationally recognised two-letter code which is embodied in the ISO 3166 list. In this country, the country domain is signified by the '.co.uk' stem. This confirms that the domain is located in the United Kingdom and is regulated by Nominet.

The country domains are registered by national naming authorities such as Nominet.uk in the UK on a first come, first served basis. They are valid for two years after which they may be renewed. Top-level country domains consist of over 240 country codes, for example: .uk (UK), .fr (France), .ie (Ireland). However, the country code is separated into sub-categories called second-level domain names, each of which relate to their type of category. These include:

- .co.uk (for commercial enterprises);

- .org.uk (for non-commercial organisations);

- .net.uk (for ISPs);

- .ltd.uk and plc.uk (for use by registered companies only).

We have noted that the effective use of generic domains can assist in the easy identification of your organisation's activities. However, there is currently a shortage of global domain names which would enable that ease of reference, for example '.arts' or '.shop'. The enlargement of global domains would undoubtedly make for more unique and meaningful web addresses available to businesses and individuals.

However, at the time of writing, there is an international dispute over how the Internet domain name system ought to be run. This followed initial proposals by the United States which were challenged by other international groups concerned at the apparent hijacking of authority over the Internet by the United States.

There are currently seven new top-level domain names proposed which are due to be released in 2000. They are:

- .web (this will be highly desirable for any business that focuses on the web);

- .shop (this may be attractive for any company operating an online retail business – prospective buyers are more likely to visit an address that ends in '.shop' than one that ends in '.com');

- .firm (this may be helpful for those businesses which have missed out on a '.com' registration);

- .info (if it is information that a website provides primarily then this may be the best domain name);

- .arts (an alternative to the '.org' address);

- .rec (this may be used by businesses providing, for example, television, sports, cinema, video, games or travel services);

- .nom (this is a personal domain name).

No names will be registered until ICANN creates the new top-level domain names and begins to accept registrations.

Are there any additional top-level generic domain names being sought?

Yes. The European Commission proposes to apply to ICANN for a new .eu domain. This is with a view to strengthening the infrastructure for e-commerce in Europe. The Financial Services Authority (FSA) is also drawing up plans whereby organisations regulated by the FSA would have a .fin domain name.

2.2.3 The importance of pre-registration searches

Why is it essential to undertake a sophisticated pre-registration search?

Many registration agents will sell a domain name without any checks other than an availability search. When your organisation requests a name, the agent will query the database of the registry or network information centre for an exact match to your name. If there is no match, they will sell your company a name.

There is a danger in adopting an overly simplistic approach to the choice of name process. It is possible to miss variations on your preferred name which might be confusing to users of the Internet. A consequence of this is that your company might inadvertently infringe someone else's rights. Alternatively, you may fail to identify existing registrations which dilute or conflict with your own intended name.

It is therefore prudent to devise a search strategy which is as effective as any trade mark or company search you may commission. The majority of organisations will commission a pre-registration search from a specialist agency offering domain name searches.

When putting in hand your search, your business should adopt a search strategy which suits its needs. For example, some companies restrict their search to names registered in the UK or which bear the '.com' suffix. Clearly, the most comprehensive approach is a worldwide search. It is also important that you decide what you wish to search for. If your company wishes to clear a name before registering it, you will need to consider:

- all names that contain elements of the character string of your preferred name;

- who the name has been registered to;

- who appears on the registration record as a named contact;
- where these people are based;
- when the name was first registered.

The record can also reveal other facts depending upon the amount of data the registry makes available. It may show the servers on which a registration is held. It is useful to see what other registrations are held on the same servers as there might be other names belonging to you or to other trade mark owning companies.

Our search agents have identified a conflicting registration with our company name which we consider is a deliberate infringing registration. What should we do?

If you believe the registration is an infringing registration undertaken by a pirate for profit, you might wish to undertake further searches. First, you can search for other registrations which use the same character string. The infringer might have registered variations of your name or mark. This will reveal if they are pirates with a record of infringement. In this instance, your organisation might then be able to join with other infringed companies to reduce the cost of action. This was a strategy pursued by Marks & Spencer in the One in a Million case[2] (see section 2.5 below). Second, your business can also search to establish what other registrations are held on the servers and who owns those servers.

2.2.4 Perfecting the registration

As soon as your company is secure in the knowledge that its choice of name is free, you should act swiftly to obtain it. It is estimated that a domain name is registered every few seconds so a delay can invalidate your searches.

What points should we consider at the stage of making the registration?

Remember, the reason for placing your business online is commercial benefit. It is important that you keep that aim in mind at all stages of perfecting your Internet presence.

The following are some of the considerations you should address:

- In this country, anyone can register a name under the '.co.uk' suffix. However, if you wish to register under the '.plc.uk' or '.ltd.uk' suffix you must be that plc or limited company. Thus, you must supply your company registration number. In addition, the domain name applied for must match, character for character, your company registration.
- It is prudent to check the terms and conditions operated by the network information centre which your search agent has selected. When you engage the

services of an agent, you should ask them to supply you with the terms of the network information centre because you should know the answers to the following questions:

– How much do they charge for a registration in the first year?

– How much do they charge for renewals?

– How many years do you pay in advance?

– What is their policy for disputes?

– How much data on your organisation will they make available?

– What certification will they provide you with to confirm that you have a contract with them?

One of the principal attractions of the Internet is the ability it offers your business to access a global customer or client base. With that aim in mind you must consider the complications which can arise at all stages of your e-commerce strategy. These potential difficulties are present at the registration stage just as they are at later intervals of online operations. We have highlighted above the differing requirements of other jurisdictions over choice of domain name. They also exist at the point of perfecting your name registration. There are currently over 180 network information centres and approximately 120 of them have pre-registration requirements.[3] Some countries limit applicants to one name per company. Others insist that the name you register must be close to your company name. Italy, for example, requires your company to be a member of a Chamber of Commerce.

– When you place your order for a registration, you should insist that the registration agent puts your name on the registration record and not their own. Check the domain name records and verify that the domain is operational before paying the agents.

Is it possible to cancel or surrender our chosen name at any time?

Yes. Your company may cancel or suspend its domain name before the expiration of the registration period by completing a surrender form. Transfer of your domain name may be made by completing the transfer form on the reverse of the registration certificate. Both your company and the new registrant should notify the registrar of the change.

2.2.5 Managing your domain name portfolio

It may well be that your organisation wishes to acquire a number of domain names. This may be because you operate a series of different businesses in this country, or alternatively you may have multiple representation in other jurisdictions as discussed above. Wherever your business owns several domain names consideration must be given to managing them. Domain names need to be hosted and renewed. Your company might wish to sell or transfer them or point them from one site to another.

What form should my management of our domain name activities take?

First, you should establish a database of your domain name registrations. This will include renewal dates and who appears on the registration records. Some domain name registration agents operate an Internet-based system which allows their larger clients to log on to a secure site with a password and view records. Requests for changes or new registrations can be e-mailed on a form that is sent to the client and then on to the registration agent.[4]

Next, your company should ensure it has a system for renewals. It is unfortunate when your organisation has been beaten to a name by someone with a right to use it. However, it would be mismanagement to have a name suspended or deleted because a renewal date was missed. The situation may worsen if your original domain name has been featured on your company publicity. In addition, it is a fact of business life that employees come and go. Therefore, you should constantly review your registration records to ensure that they feature role as opposed to named contacts. Thus, if a named individual leaves your organisation a renewal reminder will find the role contact, for example RenewalsManager@ABC.co.uk.

Consider systematic, professional monitoring of your domain name. Global domain name watching is important. There is little sense in registering a name if you have no desire to protect it.

2.2.6 Domain name disputes

The potential for dispute in a system of name registration with the attendant limitations occasioned by the very technical form the Internet takes is great. The likelihood of disputes arising is exacerbated by the speed at which the medium has developed and has been recognised for its commercial opportunity. There are many organisations in this country which, had they been closer to the evolvement of the Internet, would have secured their chosen name at an earlier stage. This brief delay in some instances has led to that name having prior registration. It is thus unsurprising that where commercial interests are significant, conflict over domain names is a growing area of litigation. One problem is that, for example, trade marks are geographically limited while domain names are not.

It is inevitable that a system such as the Internet which is growing exponentially and which is still in relative infancy will produce conflicts. Out of a potential for chaos must come order. We noted that in this country a company called Nominet.uk is responsible for maintaining the domain name registry. It is with the likelihood of periodic dispute in mind that Nominet.uk Limited operates a Dispute Resolution Service (see below).

The Nominet.uk Dispute Resolution Service[5]

How does Nominet.uk's Dispute Resolution Service operate?

It is helpful to consider the Nominet procedure by reference to a supposed question.

My company strongly believes it has a prevailing right to use a domain name.

Nominet will intervene to assist you. This assistance takes three forms:

- investigation;
- formal action under the rules; and
- the Nominet Alternative Dispute Resolution Service.

Investigation

Nominet will first seek to establish whether a mutually acceptable resolution to the dispute can be found. They will offer the impartial help of senior executive staff of Nominet.uk.

Formal action under the rules

Nominet.uk may suspend delegation of an Internet domain name in certain circumstances. This is occasioned by their authority under the rules for '.uk' domains and sub-domains. Typically, the dispute will have arisen because a third party has drawn Nominet.uk's attention to a potential confusion. Usually that third party would inform Nominet.uk that in their view your domain name and that of the other party is being used in a manner likely to cause confusion to Internet users. However, there are other more objective circumstances which may lead to the suspension of your domain name, for example where it is drawn to Nominet.uk's attention that a domain name is administered in a way likely to endanger operation of the domain name system. This is the system that keeps track of domain names and which computers they are on, and also routes mail from one computer to another.

If investigation does not lead to an acceptable resolution of your dispute Nominet.uk will consider the evidence assembled during their investigation. It will then determine whether the delegation of the domain name should be suspended.

We are dissatisfied with Nominet's decision to suspend delegation of our desired domain name. What can we do?

In this instance, you can request Nominet.uk to refer the suspension to an independent expert for a written recommendation that Nominet.uk should confirm or revoke its decision. Nominet.uk maintains a list of independent experts. They are consulted on a rota basis. This is subject always to any conflicts of interest identified by the expert in question. The expert will be provided with copies of all letters, faxes, e-mails and notes pertinent to your claims. Nominet.uk will also send a short statement confirming the background, timing and implementation of its decision.

At this stage your company, and all other interested parties will be informed by Nominet.uk of the referral to the expert. Your company will be provided with copies of relevant documents. The expert will invite both you and your opponent to make one written submission within 14 days of the expert's receipt of all the documents you have supplied them. Neither your organisation or your opponent will have the right to call for a hearing before the expert at which witnesses would be examined; however, the expert may invite each of you to appear before them. The expert would then issue their written recommendation to Nominet.uk accompanied with reasons. Copies will be provided to you no later than one month after the expert receives the background correspondence.

What happens next?

Immediately on receipt of the expert's recommendation Nominet.uk will reconsider its earlier decisions in your case to suspend the delegation of your desired domain name. A final decision will be made and confirmed to all interested parties.

We are still dissatisfied with Nominet.uk 's final decision. How do we proceed?

Upon learning of your stance, Nominet.uk will inform you and your opponents of the Nominet.uk Alternative Dispute Resolution Service. This service is administered by the Centre for Dispute Resolution (CDR).[6] Details of the services will be sent to you. If you or your adversary refuse to enter into a mediation agreement, or mediation does not resolve your dispute, you can always seek advice from your solicitors. That legal advice will be based on the merits of pursuing your case by litigation in the courts or in arbitration if your opponent consents.

Nominet.uk Alternative Dispute Resolution Service

How is the Nominet.uk Alternative Dispute Resolution Service administered?

The process is a form of mediation whereby you and the party with whom you are in disagreement agree to a neutral third party acting as arbiter. That intermediary will assist you to reach a negotiated settlement agreement. The mediation fees and expenses will normally be met by you and the other parties. The whole process is intended to avoid the delay, expense and confrontation associated with court litigation and arbitration. Even under the new streamlined civil litigation court process pursuant to the recommendations of Lord Woolf,[7] litigation in this country should only be entered into if it is absolutely necessary.

Mediation is not binding. There is no commitment to settle and the mediator has no power to impose resolution on the parties. However, when an agreement is reached it may be documented and signed by the parties. The effect of this is the creation of an enforceable contract at the option of you or your opponent which can be used in court.

Cybersquatting

What is cybersquatting?

This is where an individual or company registers a well-known trade mark as a domain name. The issue in this country was first given legal efficacy in what has become known as the Harrods case.[8] The facts of this case serve to illustrate the issue and the decision provided an early indication as to how the English courts treat the practice.

The facts of the Harrods case

The well-known department store Harrods discovered that a Mr Michael Lawrie had registered the domain name Harrods.com with the American domain name registrars NSI (see section 2.2.2). Harrods was able to persuade NSI to suspend the name but Lawrie refused to transfer the name to Harrods. Since Mr Lawrie and Harrods were both resident in England a court action was commenced in England and NSI confirmed that it would comply with any decision the English court should make. Harrods alleged that Mr Lawrie and various other defendants had infringed Harrods trade marks and engaged in passing off (see Chapter 7) and common law conspiracy.

Harrods applied for Summary Judgment. This is a procedure in English law where a plaintiff applies for judgment in its favour on the ground that, notwithstanding the filing of a defence, the defendant has no real defence to the claim or to a particular part of the claim. Ultimately, one of the defendants consented to a court order being made which was satisfactory to Harrods and the remaining defendants failed to continue their defence.

However, the issue of cybersquatting was clarified and the practice of domain name piracy was effectively buried in this country in the One in a Million decision.[9] At the time of writing, this case is the highest considered United Kingdom case on domain names.

What were the facts of the One in a Million case?

The case concerned the business of One in a Million Limited. One in a Million are dealers in Internet domain names. They register names with organisations including Nominet and sell them to potential users, very much in the same way as company registration agents. The company had, without the plaintiff's consent, registered the plaintiff's names and trade marks as Internet domain names and then sought to sell them. Such was the significance of the principle and the clear need to have the English courts stamp on the issue determined once and for all that Marks & Spencer's action was supported by J Sainsbury plc, Virgin Enterprises Limited, Ladbrokes plc, British Telecommunications plc and Securicor Cellular Radio Limited. All these plaintiffs claimed that the defendant's activities constituted threats of passing off and infringement and that they were entitled to injunctive relief. The defendant acknowledged that the trade names of all these businesses are well-known brand names with substantial goodwill attaching to them. One in a Million had registered sainsbury.com, virgin.org, labrokes.com, britishtelecom.co.uk, britishtelecom.net and britishtelecom.com in addition to marks&spencer.com. The defendant acknowledged that it had registered domain names with a view to making a profit. This might be achieved either by a sale to the owners of the goodwill and securing a considerable payment using the blocking effect of the registration. Alternatively, they may have sold them to collectors. The defendant maintained that this would not amount to passing off or a threat to pass off. Having lost at first instance, the Court of Appeal dismissed the appeal of One in a Million and granted a permanent injunction. The court held that the registration of a distinctive name such as marks&spencer clearly made a false representation to persons who consulted the register, that the registrant had connection or was associated with the name registered. This therefore did amount to passing off in law.

What is the position in English law in the light of the Harrods and One in a Million cases?

The judgments make clear the attitude of the English courts to the practice of cybersquatting. The abusive activities of domain name pirates and cybersquatters who seek to take speculative advantage of the goodwill established in well-known marks is unlawful. They reinforce the view that domain names clearly perform a trade mark function and that trade mark owners can legitimately expect to have their rights protected on the Internet. If an organisation registers the names of organisations without their consent with a view to making a profit from their use, this constitutes both passing off and trade mark infringement. In such a case, the appropriate legal remedy is the assignment of the offending names to the organisations concerned. If, however, the organisation already has an operational website this assignment is irrelevant. In such instance, damages for any loss occasioned as a consequence of the misuse would be payable by the defendant.

If my organisation wishes to register a domain name, what should we do?

It is important to appreciate that the two cases reviewed relate to high profile brands known to all. Nonetheless, the legal principles settled by these cases apply to lesser known marks which are entitled to the same degree of protection in law. Therefore, when registering a domain name, you should undertake trade mark searches to avoid conflict with trade mark owners.

We have undertaken a trade mark search and discovered a potential conflict with a registered mark. How should we proceed?

You should seek agreement with the trade mark owners to avoid potential passing off problems. If it can be established that there is no likelihood of passing off or trade mark infringement, the domain name should be safe for you to use. While no businesses should attempt to blackmail a trade mark owner the converse situation of intimidation by those owners when there is in fact no likelihood of passing off should likewise not be tolerated.

2.3 YOUR WEBSITE DEVELOPMENT AGREEMENT

Before your goods and services can be marketed or sold, your company will need to establish a website as its shop window to the world. Typically, both the design of your site and its establishment on the Internet are contracted out to a third party.

2.3.1 Specification and initial design

Your company will provide text, graphics and other material to enable the website developer to produce for your website a specification or a baseline for the succeeding phrases. This may be a description of the website and/or storyboards for the appearance of various sections of the site. In addition, it will set out whether certain sections of the site are to have registered access. Further, the question of whether your site should work both with and without frames or whether there should be a text-only version should be established.

In common with the development of software, website development is very specialised. Thus, your company will have to rely almost entirely upon the developer's skill and judgment. This expertise will not only cover advice on the layout and format of your website, but also its operation, for example the speed at which it appears on screen when accessed and 'hyperlinked' to other websites. Moreover, the ease with which your goods can be accessed, ordered and paid for over the Internet is determined by the developer's skills.

To ensure your website is an effective vehicle for the promotion and sale of your goods and services, you must insist upon extensive warranties on the part of the developer.

What is a website agreement?

This is the agreement which will govern the contractual relationship between your organisation and the company or developer you select to design, develop and install your website. The agreement also details the support, updating and other services which the developer would typically provide. The terms of the agreement will apply to all dealings between the developer and your organisation.

That relationship is clearly important. The developer provides the means to enable your business to conduct its e-commerce strategy. In common with all other business relationships, the potential for dispute or misunderstanding nonetheless exists. The settling of a website development agreement provides certainty in this fundamental element of your online presence.

It is useful to consider the ambit which the agreement should cover. However, the provisions reviewed herein will require specific tailoring and full advice should be sought from your solicitors. The following serves only as a guide to the principal provisions one would expect to see included in a website development agreement.

2.3.2 Typical provisions

Your organisation's requirements and selection of server

The developer should undertake to be solely responsible for properly ascertaining your requirements for your website through discussions with all your relevant personnel. In addition, they should select the best Internet service provider and server(s). The developer will also select and supply the proper software and ensure that all relevant software licences are executed by the software owner.

The agreement will also ensure that a proper specification is drawn up for any bespoke software developed for your business.

What is bespoke software?

This is any software program, manuals or other documentation written by the developer for you which fulfils your requirements for your website to operate efficiently and effectively on the website server (and any other server(s) to which the website server may be linked) recommended by the developer.

It is important to note that the copyright in the bespoke software will belong to your organisation as the client.

Installation and acceptance testing of your website

The developer will code the text, graphics and other material provided by your company and create your website. The contract may subdivide this process into further stages and you should expect to be kept informed of progress. The contract may provide for periodic inspection of the work or for remote access to the work in progress to be permitted.

This may be carried out in a variety of ways but typically the developer will create a prototype site on a closed system which your company will test. There may then be further live testing on the Internet but with the site hidden under a dummy name until it is ready to be made public.

You should agree suitable dates for running 'acceptance tests'. Upon passing each test to your satisfaction, the developer should deliver to you a copy of the website files, source code, object code, software listings and all other multimedia, audio visual or other material relative to the website and bespoke software.

The developer should also deliver into escrow a copy of the code, listings, and information relating to its own and any third-party software which is included in your website and server. This should be recorded in an escrow agreement which will form part of the main agreement with your company.

Only when all acceptance tests have been completed to your satisfaction should you sign a final acceptance certificate.

What if our website and/or servers failed to pass any of the acceptance tests or do not meet our requirements?

You should give the developer the opportunity to rectify, replace and retest at the developer's cost. In addition, the developer should pay an agreed rate of (liquidated) damages for every day, week or month beyond the agreed timetable that the acceptance tests are late.

If the website or server(s) still fail to satisfy our needs, what can we do?

The developer will be liable to immediately refund any monies you have paid for the rejected website and any monies you have paid to the developer for any website server hosting.

Price and payment

The agreement will specify the price for website design and development. It is common for payment to be staggered over various agreed intervals. For example, a percentage of the fee might be paid 14 days after you have signed the acceptance certificate following successful completion of the 'look and feel' test and delivery of the material referred to above. A further percentage might be paid 14 days after completion of the 'live running' test.

The developer's training, consultancy and project management

The developer should provide you with training, consultancy and project management services. These will relate to the design, development, installation and customisation of your website. This assistance might be whole or for a specified period. Usually the assistance will cover the warranty period (see below). Thereafter, the assistance will be provided only to the extent that your organisation may from time to time request. The developer should also provide maintenance and support for your website and any bespoke software for the warranty period.

The developer's undertakings

The developer should undertake not to send out any unsolicited e-mails (spamming – see section 2.4 below) for itself or on your behalf without your express prior written consent. In light of the legal treatment of spamming they should indemnify you for any claims arising from any unauthorised activity of this kind. Similarly, the developer should not 'frame' your material (see section 2.7 below). Finally, the developer should not 'link' to any third party's site without your prior written consent (see section 2.6 below).

   The agreement should also specify that the developer should not itself use, or make available, any information posted to your website by users. Such unauthorised information might include the number of users, regularity of use, names, addresses, e-mail, phone or fax addresses or any other details which are highly confidential to your business.

Warranty

The developer should warrant that the website accepted by you will be free from defects and entirely suitable for your business requirements. The agreement should specify that the developer will also rectify any significant defects or deficiencies within an agreed period of notification after their discovery. In view of the nature of the medium, this might be within a matter of hours. The developer should also warrant that it will be in a position to support your website for a period of usually not less than two years.

The warranty in the agreement should also require the developer to state that the website server(s) and software (including bespoke software) will be free from all viruses, worms, trojan horses and other software contaminants. The developer should warrant that it has used the most comprehensive and up-to-date virus checker. Any loss or damage your organisation suffers should be indemnified by the developer.

It is important to also include a warranty that the developer is insured for all liabilities specified in the website development agreement.

Your organisation's copyright, trade marks and other intellectual property rights

In Chapter 7 we will examine the law relating to your intellectual property rights as they relate to the Internet. The development agreement should cover these rights. Your company's corporate know-how used or which subsists in your website should be expressed to be your sole property. This information will include all documentation, flowcharts, drawings, specifications and other data which is created for the purpose of the agreement. The developer should hold a copy of these for support purposes only. The agreement should specify that all rights in graphics and text which are necessary to enable you to reproduce and create derivative works from the website are within your ownership.

It is important that the developer warrants that it has obtained all necessary consents, approvals and licences for any third-party intellectual property rights.

In section 2.2 above we considered your domain names. The agreement should state that all domain names belong solely and exclusively to your company. The developer's use of your domain names must be limited to the development and (if applicable) hosting of your website.

Your company's confidential information and security

It will be necessary for your company to provide information, specifications, design, material and other data to the developer to enable them to produce your website. The agreement should specify that any such information relating to your business is confidential. For maximum protection it would be prudent to have the developer sign a separate confidentiality agreement.

2.4 SPAMMING

What is spamming?

Electronic mail is perhaps the most effective online promotion for your organisation. It can also be the most controversial. One of the attractions of the medium is that you can collect the names and e-mail addresses of people who send your organisation mail. These messages can be categorised in a database, and large numbers of queries can be answered in an automated fashion. Another commercial tactic is to offer users the chance to join your mailing list. In this way, they can receive special offers, details of your company's new merchandise or industry updates if yours is a service business. However, the unfettered use of such techniques must be guarded against. The Internet world has ascribed the sending of unwanted electronic junk mail a new name – spamming.

Spamming exists primarily because it costs no more to send an e-mail to 1 000 000 people than to one. The technological means to effect spamming is readily available and inexpensive. All that is needed is a mailing list and programs which collect e-mail addresses from newsgroups, online services and Internet service providers. The problem is made worse by the fact that organisations are responsible for transmitting unsolicited e-mails. Such organisations often route their messages through other mailboxes, often the central e-mail servers of Internet service providers. The unwanted messages often include a website address where their customers can respond. Since the path of the message is itself fraudulent, any unfavourable e-mail from the recipient is delivered to the Internet service provider's server and not the spammer. The sheer volume of spamming can block Internet service providers' services rendering impossible the normal carriage of traffic to and from their customers.

How does the law treat spamming?

At the time of writing, there is no reported English court decision dealing with spamming. It is highly likely the practice will be frowned upon by the courts and therefore your company should not engage in spamming.

How does the government propose to treat the problem of spamming?

The government issued a Consultation Paper in 1998 seeking views on whether it should take any measures to regulate unsolicited e-mails.[10] The majority of feeling was to allow the industry to take effective voluntary measures, but the government should keep a watching brief and be ready to take legislative action if necessary. The government has decided to follow this approach and work with industry, and rely on existing measures. The EU Distance Selling Directive (97/7/EC) (see section

2.8 below) contains provisions requiring member states to enable consumers to register their objection to receiving unsolicited e-mails sent for the purpose of distance selling and to have their objections respected. The Directive does not apply to business-to-business transactions and certain contracts are excluded, including those related to financial services (the subject of a separate EU proposal). The Directive has to be implemented by 4 June 2000 and the Department of Trade and Industry plans to consult on its implementation later that year.

There are also rights under the Data Protection Act 1998 (see Chapter 10) enabling a person to give notice to the data controller that his or her data is not to be processed for the purposes of direct marketing.

2.5 META-TAGGING

Few of us speak, or write fluent HMTL (see section 2.1 above). What you see when you find the web page you are looking for may only be part of the source code for that page. It is the part that you do not see which is the subject of this section. We have considered the legal and technical problems associated with domain names in section 2.2. In this section we will review a different legal question – the misuse of meta-tags.

What are meta-tags?

Meta-tags are part of the programming language of the World Wide Web. Meta-tags provide a method by which you, as owner of a website, can stipulate in advance the references to your page that you would like to appear on the indexes produced by the 'spiders' which crawl through the web indexing the various pages for use in search engines. Meta-tags encode specific pieces of information and are often used to describe the contents of a website. When your organisation establishes its web presence your website designer will have inserted a series of key words which help describe your business. This enables web crawlers to index your website. The meta-tag is inserted in the head of your website document. Some web crawlers look for key words, others for a description. Your key words can be picked up and catalogued by search engines such as Yahoo, Alta Vista and Lycos. These search engines also pick up the key words in websites. If a key word is found in a website's meta-tag then it will normally be rated as more important by the search engine's databases. Thus, by encoding key word information in the meta-tags of a web page, you can affect how a search engine will index that page. In addition, you may decide what types of search will result in a hit to your company's website and how prominently your business pages will appear in a list of hits.

There are several types of meta-tags that are in common use. These include:

- the title of your company's web page;
- the description of your company's web page; and
- the key words of your company's website.

Example

If your business (XYZ Limited) supplies computer cabling, your website may read 'XYZ Limited: one of the UK's leading computer cable suppliers'. Among the key words included in your website by way of example might be 'cable', 'computer', 'IT', etc. These can be picked up by the search engines and categorised.

A practical point to note in this review of the principles of meta-tags is that, if your organisation intends to transact business globally by use of the Internet, you should consider using foreign words to attract overseas customers or clients. In addition, consider also the use of North American spellings to make the site more accessible to American readers.

Where do the legal problems of meta-tagging arise?

Meta-tags are the computer world's equivalent to 'invisible ink'. Internet users have discovered that by programming someone else's trade mark, product or service description into their own meta-tags, users can be led onto their own pages as opposed to the pages of the real trade mark, product or service owner. If one were to reach the offending website, there would be no indication of any of the hidden names anywhere on the page. It would only be by studying the source code for the page that one would find the elusive references. Indeed, some pages have lists of names running into thousands of words either within meta-tags or on the page themselves in text, which is the same colour as the background so that they cannot be seen. With the increasing influence of advertising on the web (see Chapter 8), it is likely that the rates, which will be chargeable for advertising space on a page, will be directly referable to the number of hits on the page. Thus, the problem is a very real one.

At the time of writing, there are no reported English legal cases which demonstrate how the English courts will deal with this form of abuse. It is therefore necessary to look to other jurisdictions when considering the issue. In the United States, there have been three recent cases which address the problem. They are helpful in illustrating the likely legal stance for present purposes and may be influential when such legal problems are brought before the English and other European courts.

Playboy Enterprises Inc. v. *Calvin Designer Label*

This case[11] concerned a website called 'Playmen' which had used the Playboy trade mark among its meta-tags. The result of such use was that it was capturing part of Playboy's market. The services provided were similar to Playboy material. The court had no difficulty in finding such behaviour to be an infringement of the plaintiff's rights. The decision was made easier as a defendant had also registered domain names including Playboy's registered trade mark, 'playboyxxx.com' and 'playmatelive.com'. The plaintiff successfully obtained an injunction compelling the defendants to cease use of any of the plaintiff's registered trade marks in its website meta-tags and its domain name.

Instituform Technologies Inc. v. *National Enviro Tech Group LLC*

This case[12] concerned the trade marks 'Instituform' and 'Institupipe'. Once again, a competitor had inserted the plaintiff's registered trade mark into the meta-tags of their website. One of the plaintiff's arguments was that such action was no different to altering a telephone company's database. So when a caller asked for the plaintiff's number it got that of the defendant's. Judgment was awarded to the plaintiff ordering the defendant to delete the mark 'Instituform' and 'Institupipe' from their meta-tags. The court order also prevented the defendant from ever using the trade marks in any of their other websites. In addition, the defendant was required to notify the search engines of the court ruling and instruct them to delete the link in their databases between the plaintiff's marks and the defendant's website.

Oppendahl & Larson v. *Advanced Concepts*

This is the third US case[13] which provides judicial guidance in advance of the issue of meta-tagging receiving consideration of the English courts. The Oppendahl & Larson case concerned an American law firm of that name. The firm specialises in registering domain names and setting up websites. The firm owned the domain name 'patents.com'. In the course of a regular check of its website it discovered that when searching the name 'Oppendahl & Larson' several unrelated sites appeared high on the hit list. Further investigation revealed six Internet businesses which included references to Oppendahl & Larson in their meta-tags. This function was an attempt by the companies to draw traffic to their sites. The law firm sued each business and the corresponding Internet service providers for unfair competition and dilution of their trade mark. The firm contended that the names were being used to erroneously signify that the websites concerned had been established with help from Oppendahl & Larson. The firm felt that the use of meta-tags to increase traffic to the infringers' websites amounted to unfair competition because it relied on and made use of the goodwill associated with the law firm's name. The plaintiff secured permanent injunctions against the defendants and prevented them from using the name in their meta-tags.

My company has discovered a competitor using meta-tags in this manner to gain commercial advantage. How are the English courts likely to deal with our problem?

The US cases reviewed above are helpful indicators of how the English courts will consider the point. However, we have to examine the question in the context of existing English legal statute and precedent.

Could our competitors' meta-tagging constitute a trade mark infringement under English law?

In England and Wales registered trade marks are protected by the Trade Marks Act 1994 (see Chapter 8). The Act covers the following:

1. use of *an identical sign* in the *course of trade* in respect of *identical goods or services*; or

2. use of an *identical sign* in respect of *similar goods or services*; or

3. use of a *similar mark* in respect of *identical or similar goods or services*.

However, 2 and 3 above are subject to a subjective test of the likelihood of confusion to the public. This includes a likelihood of the public associating the marks with the original. Thus, as soon as one leaves the realm of an identical mark in relation to identical goods one has to apply that subjective test. In answer to the question about the activities of a competitor, the critical point in trade mark infringement actions is as follows. Unless there is use of an *identical* mark in relation to *identical goods or services* there must be an *element of confusion* on the part of the customer. If that can be established the company is very likely to succeed in a claim for trade mark infringement.

Might the English courts treat meta-tagging as 'passing off'?

English law is unusual in that to date there is no general law of unfair competition unlike in many continental jurisdictions. Reliance must therefore be placed upon the common law action of 'passing off'. This action requires a number of conditions to be fulfilled before such a claim can be successfully brought. These include:

1. *reputation or goodwill* acquired by the plaintiff in his name, goods, mark, etc.;

2. misrepresentation made to the customer by the defendant which leads to *confusion or deception*; and

3. damage to the plaintiff caused by the above.

As with trade mark infringement, your customers might be subject to an element of confusion if the company contends its competitor's action constitutes 'passing off'. However, with regard to passing off a plaintiff must also show misrepresentation. The essence of the tort of passing off is a misrepresentation to the public (whether intentional or unintentional) liable to lead them to believe the goods or services offered by the representor are those of the plaintiff. However, passing off is also committed by those who put or authorise someone to put an 'instrument of deception' into the hands of others. Once again, when considering the application of English law to a twenty-first century Internet problem, in this instance meta-tagging, we need to look back to the nineteenth century. As long ago as 1880 it was said in *Singer v. Loog*:[14]

> *No man is permitted to use any mark, sign or symbol, device or other name whereby, without making a direct false representation himself to a purchaser who purchases from him, he enables such a purchaser to tell a lie or to make a false representation to somebody else who is the ultimate customer.*

In the present case, it might be argued that any misrepresentation a competitor may have occasioned is to the search engines, not to the customer. Since a machine can hardly be said to have been misled it is possible that the English courts would not regard such actions by a competitor as amounting to 'passing off'.

Conclusion

The above analysis of relevant English legal principles is necessary and helpful in examining how the courts in this country are likely to approach meta-tagging. It is most likely that the courts will look very unfavourably on a defendant using another individual's or organisation's trade mark in their meta-tags without cogent reason. Support for this view exists in the One in a Million case (see p. 23 above). The Court of Appeal stated in that case that the registration of other firms' brand names as domain names was an instrument of deception. The judges referred to the old case of *Singer v. Loog* in arriving at that conclusion. The judges likened the registration of other firms' brand names as domain names to where well-known company names have been registered at Companies House just before a merger has been officially announced. Similarly, analogy was drawn to where a company name registration is undertaken for use before a foreign company is due to open up business in the UK. Both practices have received judicial condemnation. It is likely similar reasoning could be applied in meta-tagging cases, that trade marks inserted in meta-tags are being used as instruments of deception. Meta-tagging presents yet another novel issue in the growing field of Internet litigation when new forms of technology must be evaluated under the more traditional principles of intellectual property law.

How can my company avoid becoming involved in meta-tagging disputes?

As a practical matter, most business managers responsible for commercial websites will want to take care to ensure that their meta-tags do not contain trade marks of other parties. The following should be borne in mind:

- Your business must be careful not to infringe other organisations' trade marks when establishing its website using meta-tags.

- It would also be prudent for you to undertake regular test runs to see whether other unrelated sites systematically come up when certain trade marks are entered into a search.

- If anything suspicious is found, it is straightforward to access another organisation's meta-tags to make further investigation. The source code of a site can be viewed by anyone.

- It is a commercial imperative for your business to protect its trade marks. However, care must be taken not to write letters that threaten trade mark infringement. This may result in the recipient of your threats bringing legal proceedings against your business under section 21 of the Trade Marks Act 1994 for an injunction and/or damages for any loss suffered.

2.6 LINKING TO OTHER WEBSITES

What is linking?

Linking has been called the concept on which the Internet is based. It is a feature of the Internet that is fundamental to its operation. The power of the web stems from the ability of a link to point to any document, regardless of its status or physical location. Linking was purposely built into HTML and permits the user to click on a location on the sponsor's own website. The user is then automatically connected to the third-party website without need to input any location information or consult any directory, index or search engine. A link is an embedded electronic address that points to another site and takes the user there. The electronic address is stored and, upon clicking, sends the address to the browser which moves the user to the website with that address. Thus, it enables jumping from one page to another page of a particular website and so makes 'surfing the net' possible.

How might my business use linking on our own sales website?

One of the most important features of HTML is that it can include hypertext jumps that link one part of a web page to another, one web page to another page, or one web page to another website. Your website may have a facility to enable online customers to order your goods over the Internet. If so, you would want a hotword 'order' that will jump to another page on your site for ordering products. The word 'order' will jump to the relevant ordering page if the user clicks on the hotword.

What is the commercial prejudice associated with linking?

To understand how linking can be considered an act of unfair competition in some instances one must appreciate the commercial realities of the Internet. Many companies are taking advantage of the Internet to increase sales by promoting their own goods or services, or for sponsorship or for advertising revenue (see Chapter 8). Typically, one website contracts with another website to display an advertisement. It is not surprising that the question of how to protect the commercial value of websites has become the subject of recent claims both in the United States and in this country. Clearly, for most commercial website operators seeking to reach as large an audience as possible, the ability to be located by search engines is all important. However, the link might be to a specific item on the other site and cause browsers to bypass information or advertising that the website owner would have wished all visitors to the site to see. This has a potential to diminish the ability of the site to convey the desired message. Moreover, the advertising revenue from that site could be prejudiced if it carries third-party adverts or if it affects sponsorship arrangements.

Hypertext links between websites is also commonplace on the Internet. A user may transfer from one site to another simply by clicking on highlighted text in the original site. The text is usually displayed in a different colour and is usually underlined. The user can go back to the original page using the 'back' button on their browser. Linking has benefits such as increasing the potential audience of a site but it can also bring undesired results.

How does English law treat unauthorised linking which causes prejudice?

Challenges to Internet linking are not unique to the UK. Just as the Internet itself spans the world, challenges to its technology have also arisen in other jurisdictions. In fact, at the time of writing, there is no reported English case providing precedent for how English law approaches the problem. The nearest legal jurisdiction offering guidance as to how the matter will be treated is Scotland. The case providing that guidance is *The Shetland Times Limited* v. *Wills*.[15]

What were the facts of the Shetland Times case?

The Shetland Times sued the Shetland News for copyright infringement when the latter set up hypertext links connecting its website to that of the Times. The Shetland Times' website contained online copies of articles and photographs that appeared in the printed edition of the paper. By clicking on one of the headlines in the *Shetland News* the user gained immediate access to the related text in the *Shetland Times* bypassing its front page. At the interlocutory stage[16] in October 1996, Lord Hamilton in the Court of Session granted an interim injunction against the Shetland News preventing it from linking to the Shetland Times' stories. The substantive case was due to be heard in the Court of Session. However, before the judge could make a ruling, a settlement was reached between the parties. The terms of that settlement included the following:

- the Shetland News would be permitted to link to individual stories provided they included the by-line 'a Shetland Times story' under each headline in the same or similar size; and

- alongside any such headline there was included a button showing a legible image of the Shetland Times masthead logo; and

- each of the headlines and buttons were to be hypertext links to the Shetland Times online headline page.

While both parties agreed the terms of the settlement it might be argued that Lord Hamilton's granting of the interim injunction suggests that linking providing direct access will not be permitted.

The case thus considered whether the creation of unauthorised links constitutes a breach of copyright. It is important to appreciate that while this was a case under Scottish law the decision was based on copyright legislation common to England, Scotland and Wales.

What was the legal principle which the action of linking offended?

The interim decision of the court found that the linking was a breach of copyright on the grounds that it constituted an infringement of copyright in a cable programme as defined by the Copyright, Designs and Patents Act 1988. In fact, this is arguably an artificial basis because linking does not actually involve copying.

The case does nonetheless provide an indication of the attitude of the English courts on the question of copyright infringement by hypertext links.

2.7 FRAMING

What is framing?

A variation of linking is the action of framing. In this, the remote user's web browser screen is subdivided into an assortment of windows or frames, each of which can be managed independently. Text can be scrolled up or down or, for example, a specific frame can be printed.

Framing is achieved using special provisions in the HTML language – the first step being to define a 'frame set' that physically splits the web browser's screen and allocates names to each of the specific frames. For example, a frame set might create a browser screen. With this in place, a link to another web page can be augmented by specifying in which frame the web page is to appear. Framing is primarily used to make browsing around a particular site simpler.

What is the commercial menace which framing produces?

It is also possible that framing may be used to prevent remote users from exiting a specific site when they browse pages on other sites – one merely has to present those other sites' pages within a 'frame'.

From the point of view of the site whose page is being framed, it might be unacceptable to have your page enclosed by some bizarre context, a context perhaps offensive to the content of your commercial website. Moreover, if your framed site's page is not your home page it might appear as if your framed page is being 'passed off' as being a page from the framing site. Furthermore, if your framed site's home page has paid advertising on it then the framing site is effectively bypassing those advertisements and falsifying any user's statistics of your framed site – such statistics often being used as the basis for fixing advertising rates (see Chapter 9).

How does the law treat framing?

At the time of writing there is no reported English case law on the issue. In the absence of domestic judicial guidance one is again compelled to look to other jurisdictions to see how foreign courts have approached the problem. Such a review serves as a firm indicator of how framing will be viewed by the English courts. The first major case to challenge framing was *Washington Post Co.* v. *Total News* No. 97-1190 (FDNY 1997). In that case, Total News provided a website that featured a list of 'name-brand' news services, identified by their trade marks, in a narrow column to the left, an advertising banner across the bottom right of the screen, and a content window in the upper right of the screen. When a user clicked on a news service, that news service's content appeared within the content window on the Total News website. However, when the news service's content first loaded, its advertisements were hidden by the advertising banner on the Total News website. Some of the framed sites such as CNN Interactive reacted by setting their pages to refresh when loaded so that the pages appeared in their own window without the Total News frame.

Total News provided no content or value of its own. The website merely linked to numerous alternative leading news sites. At all times, the visitors saw only the Internet address of Total News, no matter which website appeared. Advertisements framing the linked sites were sold by Total News, and were under Total News' complete control.

The Washington Post contended that the defendants' news service, violated both copyright and trade mark law. A settlement was reached, with Total News agreeing to cease the practice of framing the plaintiff's websites. However, the media companies agreed to grant Total News a 'linking licence' so that it can still hyperlink to stories on their sites provided that the hyperlinks consist only of the names of the linked sites in plain text.

A more recent case involving framing, based substantially on copyright claims, was decided by the US Court of Appeal. In the case of *Futuredontics Inc. v. Applied Anagramits Inc.*[17] it was held that a plaintiff whose website has been framed is not entitled to a preliminary injunction where there is no evidence of tangible loss of business or customer goodwill, affirming the decision of the US District Court for the Central District of California.

Applied Anagramits Inc. (AAI) operated a website whose pages were divided into frames (http://www.1800dentist.com/frame-in-dex.html). AAI created an unauthorised hyperlink to Futuredontics website that made the copyright materials on Futuredontics website appear within one of the frames of AAI's site. The balance of the page was surrounded with content supplied by AAI, including its logo and information about its business operation.

Futuredontics, which operates a dental referral service on the Internet, alleged that AAI, a licensor of marketing systems for dentists, impermissibly linked to the Futuredontics site and, in so doing, infringed Futuredontics' copyright as well as caused consumer confusion by falsely implying that Futuredontics was a licensee of AAI. The District Court rejected both claims, finding that the balance of hardship was not in the plaintiff's favour. On appeal, the appellate court affirmed, finding that Futuredontics had failed to show how, if at all, the framed link caused a tangible loss of business or customer goodwill.

It may well be that before the English courts are able to consider the issue of framing the technical progress on the Internet will outpace the legal threat which the practice presents.

It is fortunate from a pure commercial perspective that the advancement of technology is itself bringing a potential remedy. One means of preventing an infringement suit from occurring is for the web page owner to install web page protecting software. This can be used to design a web page to accept only those resource locator requests originating at a particular address. All other URLs which are referred to the web page return only the 'not found' message. This mechanism greatly increases a web page owner's control over his or her page.

Technology also poses other solutions by making it possible for a website owner to implement the use of passwords and registrations to refrain users from accessing a specific web page.

2.8 THE DISTANCE SELLING DIRECTIVE

The Distance Selling Directive was adopted by the European Parliament and Council in May 1997 and is due for implementation in 2000.[18]

What is the Directive designed to achieve?

It is intended to protect consumers against some of the risks involved in distance selling. In this country consumers have certain rights when they enter into contracts which have been negotiated away from business premises. Thus even where a contract has been concluded, in some instances a party can extract itself from the contract without penalty.[19]

What is the definition of a 'distance contract'?

The definition is as follows:

> *Any contract concerning goods or services concluded between a supplier and consumer under an organised distance sales or service provision scheme run by the supplier, who, for the purpose of the contract, makes exclusive use of one or more means of distance communication up to and including the moment at which the contract is concluded.*

The key to the applicability of the Directive is a contract where the supplier and the consumer do not come face to face prior to the conclusion of the contract.

Does the Directive apply to Internet sales?

Yes. It will make significant changes in the practice of those who use the Internet to sell goods and services to European consumers.

Does the Directive only relate to contracts within the European Union?

Yes. It was introduced to encourage and increase confidence in such methods of selling and also harmonise laws in all member states so that all European consumers have equality of access to goods and services in other member states.

The Internet of course by its nature will require parties to a contract to negotiate and conclude their agreement from anywhere in the world. The Distance Selling Directive will thus apply to many e-commerce transactions.

What prior information need we provide to our online customer under the Directive?

Article 4 of the Directive specifies that prior to the conclusion of any distance contract a consumer must be provided with the following information. This detail should be included on your website.

- Your company's identity must be supplied. If your contract requires payment in advance, your address should be displayed.

- The principle characteristics of your goods or services should be specified.

- All prices including taxes should be specified.

- Delivery costs must be clear, as should all payment arrangements.

- The right of your customer to withdraw must be specified.

- Any costs of using the Internet as a means of distance communication must be highlighted.

Are there any contracts which fall outside the Distance Selling Directive?

Yes. Contracts for the supply of foodstuffs, beverages or other goods intended for everyday consumption supplied to the home of the consumer, to his residence, or to his workplace by regular 'round men'. Thus, Internet grocery shopping will not be subject to the Directive because of the perishable nature of the goods concerned.

In addition, contracts for the provision of accommodation, transport, catering or leisure services, where the supplier undertakes, when the contract is concluded, to provide these services on a specific date or within a specific period, for example hotel and travel bookings, fall outside the scope of the Directive.

Other exceptions to the general right to withdraw include contracts:

- for the provision of services if performance has begun, with the consumer's agreement, before the end of seven working days;

- for the supply of goods or services, the price of which is dependent on fluctuations in financial markets which cannot be controlled by the supplier;

- for the supply of goods made to the consumer's specifications or clearly personalised or which, by reason of their nature, cannot be returned or are liable to deteriorate or expire rapidly;

- for the supply of newspapers, periodicals and magazines;

- for gaming and lottery services.

A review of the exceptions listed above should enable you to establish whether your services offered online fall outside the Directive and thus do not allow your customer to withdraw from the contract.

2.9 YOUR WEBSITE CONTENT PROVISION AGREEMENT

Your corporate website may well take different forms. In some instances, it may sell content or information in electronic form or enable your goods to be purchased online. Alternatively, it might offer information free of charge where that data is ancillary to the sale of your goods. Typically, this would be technical information relating to your product.

In Chapter 7 we examine how your intellectual property rights can be protected on the Internet. In most cases, your company will own the copyrights and database rights in the information. If not owned, such rights will usually be sublicensed to your organisation. It is important that you define the terms of use which visitors to your site must adhere to. It will be necessary for you to grant a licence to visitors who use the information posted on your website. The terms of this licence are intended to protect your existing rights and limit your liability.

What issues should we cover in our website content provision agreement?

The scope of the licence which you are granting should be clear. Your company may expressly state that users of the information on your site should only download the data for internal business purposes or for non-commercial activities. Further distribution of your material might be restricted. This is of importance where your site generates revenue per 'hit'. Usually, your advertising can be determined by this criteria (see Chapter 8). Limiting or excluding your liability is an issue which properly has its home in your website content provision agreement. Your agreement should state that, for example, information is supplied 'as is' with no guarantees as to accuracy or completeness or fitness for purpose.

We wish to set up a secure website to provide confidential materials to our customers. What points should we consider?

While the Internet is an 'open' medium, it can be used in this way. To assist legal protection, you should ensure a confidentiality agreement is entered into with each customer before your materials are disclosed. The confidentiality agreement can of course be posted on your website and signed digitally by your customer (see Chapter 5). The confidentiality agreement should specify that it will apply each time the customer accesses or downloads your material. The material you supply online should also be clearly marked 'confidential' and expressly refer to your confidentiality agreement. Access to your material must be restricted by the use of encryption and passwords.

2.10 THE WEBSITE HOSTING AGREEMENT

2.10.1 Background

When your organisation elects to pursue its e-commerce strategy it will, *inter alia*, require that its website is hosted on a server. Website hosting is merely the storage of a website and website material on a server. Typically, the server belongs to an Internet service provider ('ISP'). As the ISP is in control of the server they will wish to ensure that the material contained on your website and the material to which your site is linked is not unlawful. This is because your ISP may incur liability in a variety of ways. Civil liability may result if your site contains, for example, defamatory information (see section 6.3 below) or pirated software. Criminal sanction may arise if, for example, money laundering activity is present on a website.

Clearly, your organisation will not be engaged in any such activity. Nonetheless, it is increasingly common for ISPs to require website owners to enter into a website hosting agreement.

What are the typical provisions found in a website hosting agreement?

The following are some of the provisions one would expect to find in the agreement. The list is not, however, exhaustive. At the time of writing, there are no global laws harmonising the standards which should apply to website content, although ISPs have developed codes of conduct laying down basic rules and standards applicable to websites they host. Violation of these codes will entitle the ISP to immediately bar access and remove websites from their server.

■ The agreement will clarify that the ISP ('the host') will provide you with a dedicated server computer which is integrated into the World Wide Web via the Internet.

■ Details of hosting fees and related charges will be set out. Usually, fees are charged on a monthly basis and failure to meet the same will result in the suspension or disconnection of the hosting service.

■ Your organisation will be required to confirm that all information and activity is legal, decent and honest.

■ Data protection legislation must be adhered to (see Chapter 10) in order that the collection of personal information is not traded or disclosed illegally.

■ Distance selling requirements must be complied with (see section 2.8 above).

■ Spam (see section 2.4 above) must not be sent nor should trojan horses, viruses or other disruptive programs or devices.

■ Your organisation will be solely responsible for the accuracy of its own material.

■ The host will want you to acknowledge that the host may be required by a law enforcement agency to monitor your website content and traffic (see Regulation of Investigatory Powers Act 2000).

■ The host will want an indemnity against all liability, damages, losses and claims which result from your unlawful website content.

■ Usually the host will use its reasonable endeavours to keep server downtime to a minimum. However, it will not warrant that the hosting service or server will be continuously available.

■ The host will require you to acknowledge that copyright, trade marks, patents and other intellectual property rights developed or used in connection with the hosting service will be the host's sole property.

■ In connection with intellectual property rights, the host will want to be indemnified against liability for your organisation's infringement of other third-party intellectual property rights. This indemnity will also cover your linking (see section 2.6 above) or framing (see section 2.7 above).

■ The circumstances surrounding termination of the agreement will be set out. Termination will, for example, be triggered at the instance of the host if your organisation is in breach of the terms of the agreement or enters into compulsory or voluntary liquidation or has a receiver appointed over its undertaking.

CHECKLIST: HOW TO SET UP YOUR E-COMMERCE BUSINESS

■ Do you understand how to search for and secure a domain name and the issues you should consider?

■ Do you appreciate the distinction between legitimate conflict over a choice of domain names and cybersquatting?

■ Have you a properly drafted website development agreement with your website designer?

■ Do you understand how the law treats meta-tagging?

■ Have you obtained consent from any organisation to whose website your company would like to link to its own site?

■ Do you know whether the Distance Selling Directive applies to your online operation?

■ Has your company negotiated a formal website hosting agreement?

NOTES

1. The Internet address <u>sun.co.uk</u> in fact belongs to Sun Microsystems, the computer company.

2. *Marks & Spencer plc and others* v. *One in a Million Limited* [1998] 4 All ER 476 CA. 23 July 1998.

3. Nicholas Wood (1998) 'Securing domain name registrations', *Computers and Law*, August/September.

4. For example, see Netsearchers International Limited's website at <u>www.netsearchers.co.uk</u>.

5. Based on the Nominet UK Dispute Resolution Service at <u>www.nic.uk</u>.

6. The Centre for Dispute Resolution (CDR) has been appointed to provide accredited intermediaries for Nominet UK at a reduced rate. They also administer the Nominet Alternative Dispute Resolution Service. The organisation is an independent non-profit-making body whose aims are supported by the CBI, the DTI and the IOD. They offer a free telephone advice line for parties interested in taking an Internet domain name dispute to mediation.

7. The Woolf reforms introduced in April 1999 represent the most significant overhaul of the civil litigation court process in England and Wales for over a century. They are designed to expedite litigation, reduce costs and foster an environment of disclosure and cooperation between opponents. The emphasis is also on seeking resolution prior to a full trial between the parties.

8. The Harrods case – unreported. See Gardner (1997) 'The Harrods case: protecting your name on the Internet', *Computers and Law*, April/May, p. 23.

9. See note 2 above.

10. *Promoting Electronic Commerce*, consultation on draft legislation and the government's response to the Trade and Industry Committee's report, July 1999.

11. *Playboy Enterprises* v. *Calvin Designer Label*, 1985F Supp 1218 [ND Col Ol 1997].

12. *Instituform Technologies* v. *National Enviro Tech Group*, NO97-2064 [EBLa August 26 1997].

13. *Oppendahl & Larson* v. *Advanced Concepts*, NO97-CV-1592 [D Colo December 19 1997].

14. *Singer* v. *Loog* (1880) 18 ChD 395–412. Cited with approval by Lord MacNaughton in *Camel Harebelting* (1896) AC 199 215–16.

15. *The Shetland Times* v. *Wills* [1997] SCT 669, OH; *Times*, 21 January.

16. A court hearing which takes place before a full trial.

17. *Futuredontics Inc.* v. *Applied Anagramits Inc.* 9th Cir, No. 97-56711 1998.

18. Directive 97/7/EC of the European Parliament and of the Council of 20 May 1997.

19. For example, where the Mail Order Protection Scheme applies and in relation to certain consumer credit agreements. See Consumer Protection (Cancellation of Contracts Concluded Away from Business Premises) Regulations 1987.

3

How to form an electronic contract

The Internet represents a triumph of technology over the bonds which hitherto prevented instantaneous communication on a truly global scale.

Nonetheless the medium exists in a multi-jurisdictional world which operates with multifarious legal and cultural constraints. The technology has the potential to transform the manner in which commerce is transacted. In time, the universal adoption of a medium offering so much may well shape those national regulations drawing them together in so far as they relate to online business.

In the meantime we must consider the legal efficacy of the Internet in the context of English law. The necessity of ensuring your online commercial dealings are indeed governed by English law is considered at section 3.5 below. As the medium thus fits within an established legal framework so it is necessary to understand the process of contract formation. Such an appreciation is critical to online business but the sheer openness of the system can cause problems. As we shall see, there are, however, some precedents and guidelines from an older technology.

3.1 PRE-CONTRACT CONSIDERATIONS

A contract is founded on agreement. In its purest form agreement arises from offer and acceptance. One person makes an offer, another person accepts that offer. English law, however, demands four elements to constitute a legally enforceable contract. They are:

- offer;
- acceptance;
- consideration; and
- an intention to create legal relations.

For the purposes of this book we shall examine only the principles of offer and acceptance.

3.2 OFFER

An offer is a proposition put by one person (or persons) to another person (or persons) coupled with an intimation that he is willing to be bound to that proposition. The offeror (that is, the person who makes the offer) may make his offer to a particular person or to a group of persons or, as is the case with the Internet, to the whole world. He may make his offer in writing or in spoken words or by conduct. Thus, the offer may take any form between an elaborate document with numerous clauses and sub-clauses and an everyday act of conduct, such as a bus driver pulling up at a bus stop. The intimation that the offeror is willing to be bound need not be stated in words (written or spoken); it may be, and frequently is, inferred from the nature of the offeror's proposition or from the circumstances in which the proposition is made.

When you make an offer, you are expressing a desire to enter into a contract (based on specified terms and conditions) on the understanding that, if the other party accepts it, the agreement will be legally binding. Offers can be made using virtually any form of communication – by post, fax, telex, telephone – and now by electronic mail and the Internet.

Why is it vital to consider this legal explanation of what constitutes an 'offer'?

Our law states that if a reasonable person would interpret a particular action or communication as an offer (a readiness to bind oneself), it is an offer whether the party intended it or not. It is the appearance of an offer which is more important than actual intent. This is where the danger to electronic business exists. Careless online statements (see section 6.3) or poorly constructed websites can amount to making unintentional offers to the world which would result in unwanted binding legal contracts once consumers accept.

3.3 TRUE OFFER DISTINGUISHED FROM INVITATION TO TREAT

English contract law makes a distinction in a sales environment which many laymen think odd, but which is central to the formation of contractual relations.

It is necessary to distinguish a true offer from an 'invitation to treat'. The importance of the distinction is that if a true offer is made and is then accepted the offeror is bound. Conversely, if what the offeror said or did is not a true offer, the other person cannot by saying 'I accept' create a contract. That is, he cannot by saying 'I accept' bind the offeror. Important though the distinction is, it is not always easy to make.

The contrast between the two principles can best be illustrated by the use of examples common to commercial life.

3.3.1 Tenders

In connection with tenders, the distinction between an offer and an invitation to treat is reasonably clearly seen. If you ask a number of tradesmen to put in tenders for supplying you with some particular goods or services, you are not, in so doing, making an offer. Consequently, you are not bound to accept the lowest or any other tender. The position is similar where you ask one tradesman to put in an estimate for supplying particular goods or services. It is not you who makes the offer; the offer comes from the tradesman in the form of a tender or estimate.[1]

3.3.2 Display of goods for sale

The rule of law that calling for tenders is not making of an offer accords with common sense. That common sense is not so clearly satisfied with the parallel rule that the displaying of goods for sale is not the making of an offer. The rule was clarified by the Court of Appeal in 1953.[2] The court held that the display of articles on shelves was not an offer, only an invitation to treat. The offer was made by the customer taking the article to the cash desk. The courts take the same view of goods displayed in a shop window. In 1961 Lord Parker considered the point to be beyond argument. He said:

> *It is perfectly clear that according to the ordinary law of contract, the display of an article with a price on it in a shop window is merely an invitation to treat. It is in no sense an offer for sale, the acceptance of which constitutes a contract.*[3]

Incidentally, the law is the same if the article is displayed without a price on it.

3.3.3 Advertisements

The same rule applies to an advertisement placed, for example, by your company stating that you are willing to sell some goods. The general rule is that an advertisement is not an offer, merely an invitation to treat.[4] There is an exception which applies to what are known as unilateral contracts. A unilateral contract is a one-sided contract in the sense that one party binds himself by a conditional promise leaving the other party free to perform the condition or not, as he pleases.[5]

In a unilateral contract, the offeror will not know whether the contract is 'on' until the other party has performed his part. Unilateral contracts are a rare form of contract as most contracts are bilateral or multilateral.

How do we apply these long-established principles to the digital Internet?

To protect yourself from making unintentional offers, as an online merchant you need to observe the finest distinction between an offer and an invitation to treat just as you must by more traditional business means.

The Internet uses modern digital technology and ordinary telephone lines. It is not a closed system like telex and it offers much more through its interconnecting networks. Anyone with a modern computer, a modem, suitable programs and a

51

paid-up subscription to one of the Internet service providers can gain access to the system. By means of that system, a user can obtain information from websites, send messages through electronic mail, and order goods and services. Just as with telex, people can make contracts through e-mail.

How then will my company's website be treated on a legal basis?

The invitation to treat principle can be applied to online transactions, perhaps in the context of electronic mail price lists and websites. Websites are the electronic equivalent of shop windows and catalogues, advertising the description of the products and their prices. Electronic mail price lists are similarly analogous to circulars in conventional commerce. The problem is, at the time of writing, these analogies are conjecture since no English case law has yet verified websites as invitations to treat.

Thus there is no legal certainty. It is conceivable that your pre-written order forms containing your online standard terms and conditions could be construed (although it is unlikely) as offers. This would be because they are designed and written by you as the supplier.

How should we make it clear that our website does not constitute an irrevocable offer for sale of our goods or services?

To minimise the risk of an unfavourable court decision, your website and electronic mail solicitations should have disclaimers explicitly defining them to be invitations to treat, and not offers.

Why is it really so important we make the distinction and have our website make the position clear?

If the content of your website constitutes an offer then you will have no control over who you become legally bound to. This would be a commercially intolerable scenario. By the inclusion of an appropriate disclaimer you will ensure that your company has the ability to select customers or clients and manage its supply of goods or services.

For many reasons your organisation may not wish to deal with all customers from all jurisdictions. If you retain the power to accept or refuse, you can decline undesirable customers and clients without fear of being in breach of contract. In fact, if your business only ever intends to accept orders from UK-based companies, since the Internet is a global medium, you must place a notice on your website. That notice should state that the contents of your website are for UK customers or clients only.

3.4 DISCLAIMERS

What is a disclaimer?

A disclaimer or exemption clause is a term in a contract which seeks to exempt one of the parties from liability in certain events. The same principles apply to limitation clauses, that is clauses which seek to limit (rather than wholly exclude) a party's liability, and the clauses which provide that complaints must be made within a certain period of time.

An exemption clause is a perfectly legitimate device in contracts between parties of equal bargaining power, for example where a business transacts with another business. However, where the parties are unequal, such a clause may work injustice. In respect of your online contracts made within England and Wales, and in particular in respect of your contracts made with consumers, your company as a supplier of goods or services will need to take into account the provisions of various relevant statutes. Briefly, these include the following.

- *The Consumer Credit Act 1974.* This Act regulates the content of agreements for the provision of credit, sets out various procedures which must be followed to protect consumers and establishes a regime for licensing businesses which provide consumer credit or consumer hire.

- *The Consumer Protection Act 1987.* This Act imposes in certain circumstances strict liability on the manufacturer and other members of the distribution chain of defective goods which cause death or personal injury or loss or damage to property.

- *The Unfair Terms in Consumer Contracts Regulations 1994.* These apply to standard contracts entered into between the sellers or suppliers of goods or services to consumers. They introduce a general concept of 'unfairness' and terms which are found to be unfair will be unenforceable as against the consumer. The Regulations came into force on 1 July 1995.

However, the Act which has perhaps the widest application and for our purposes is most significant is the Unfair Contract Terms Act 1977 (as amended) ('UCTA'). It is instructive to consider that part of UCTA which has most relevance to our review of electronic contracts.

In order to understand the Act, it is first necessary to study two definitions in the Act, namely 'business liability' and 'deals as consumer'. This is because most of the Act applies only to business liability and because the consumer has a specially favoured status under the Act. 'Business liability' is liability arising from things done by a person in the course of business or from the occupation of business premises (see s. 1(iii)). A person 'deals as consumer' (see s. 12) if he does not make the contract in the course of a business and the other party does make the contract in the course of a business. If the contract is for the supply of goods, there is an additional point, namely that the goods must be of a type ordinarily supplied for private use or consumption.

What are the main provisions of the Act?

The principle provisions include the following:

- Liability (that is business liability) for death or personal injury resulting from negligence cannot be excluded or restricted by any contract term or notice (s. 2(i)).

- In the case of other loss or damage, a person cannot so exclude or restrict his (business) liability for negligence except in so far as the term or notice satisfies the requirement of reasonableness (s. 2(ii)). The requirement of reasonableness is that the term shall be a fair and reasonable one to be included having regard to all the circumstances which were, or ought reasonably to have been, known to or in the contemplation of the parties when the contract was made. The Act lays down guidelines for the application of the reasonableness test.

- When one party deals as consumer or on the other party's written standard terms of business that other party cannot:
  - when himself in breach of contract exclude or restrict his business liability in respect of the breach; or
  - claim to be entitled to render a contractual performance substantially different from that which s reasonably expected of him; or
  - claim to be entitled to performance at all except (in all three cases) subject to the requir onableness.

It is important to apprec does not set out a generalised prohibition of exemption clauses o equirement of reasonableness. There are many contracts to whi apply or does not fully apply such as contracts of insurance a ating to the transfer of land.

How do exemption clause in the context of our corporate website?

Your website (whether it is fc formation purposes only or as part of your electronic business to sell your goods or services) can create legal liability for your electronic commerce business in each country from which someone accesses your site. Thus, you should include disclaimers or exemption clauses in your website to try and limit your legal liability.

Can we include an 'all embracing' disclaimer?

The extent to which liability can be excluded or restricted can vary from country to country. It is simply not possible to draft a disclaimer which will work in every country in which your website can be accessed. This is not because of language variance, rather the fact that different countries permit different exclusions. As we have seen above, under English law it is not possible to exclude liability for death or personal injury caused by negligence. Nor is it possible to exclude liability for defamation. Thus, your disclaimer may minimise your risk of legal liability but whether a court would uphold your attempt to exclude liability will depend on the circumstances.

3.5 GOVERNING LAW

The issue of governing law is very important. The principle difficulty presented by the Internet is that it effectively abolishes geographical boundaries.

The Internet environment is essentially global. Many observers interpret that as meaning it is essentially location-less whereas in fact it means exactly the opposite. Far from being a place without locations, cyberspace – the global environment of e-commerce – is actually a place with multiple locations. The global environment of cyberspace is a place without borders, not a place without locations – and that is where the problem starts. Where a dispute arises on the Internet, a problem exists not because there is no law, nor even because there is an unwillingness to apply the law, but because there is no clear law about which country's law should be applied.

What happens if our electronic contract does not specify which law applies?

Where no governing law is referred to in a contract, the English courts will decide on what law should apply according to the provisions of the Contracts (Applicable Law) Act 1990. This Act provides a 'proper law of the contract' doctrine. Under the Act, the applicable law is that with which the transaction has the closest connection. However, in certain circumstances with respect to consumer contracts, the applicable law will be that in which the consumer has his 'habitual residence'. The circumstances could cover a foreign consumer responding to an advertisement on your website. If foreign courts are presented with a dispute under your contract, they may apply different rules for deciding what is the governing law. This might be the law of the place of contracting or the law of the place of performance.

What are some of the circumstances when habitual residence criteria in a consumer contract will be applied?

First, they will be applied if in that country the conclusion of the contract was preceded by a specific invitation addressed to him or by advertising and he has taken in that country all the steps necessary on his part for the conclusion of the contract. Alternatively, they will be applied if the other party or his agent received the consumer's order in that country.

The governing law of a disclaimer is normally the one in which the web page is accessed by your customers. While its legal effect cannot be guaranteed it may be prudent for you to provide that your online customer accepts the law which governs the disclaimer (i.e. English law).

It is also necessary to bring your disclaimer to the attention of your Internet customer. It should not be included on a separate legal page which your online customer can visit as an option. The following are some suggestions for displays:

- on the web page which contains your product or services information;

- on the entry page which requires a visitor to acknowledge before gaining entry to the rest of your website;

- a prominent link entitled 'Product Disclaimer', which should be placed at various places on your site.

Are there any complicating factors?

Yes. When choosing to include a governing law clause in your electronic terms and conditions, there is another issue you need to bear in mind. Some consideration needs to be given to the enforceability of any judgment of, for example, the English courts against your defaulting customer. If a person has a place of business in the same country as the court giving the judgment there is no problem. However, if this is not the case then one must establish the availability of reciprocal enforcement treaties between the country in which the court is situated and the country in which your potentially recalcitrant customer is based. Between countries in the EU there is not such a problem with reciprocity of enforcement. This is because of the application of the Brussels Convention. It may well be that your company decides to make it clear on its website that products it is offering over the Internet are only available to order online from those countries where you know you will not experience problems with enforcement and refuse to accept such orders online from individuals in other countries.

Another issue to consider when including a governing law clause is the following. The Internet presents problems in knowing from which jurisdiction your customer is in fact accessing your site. Your choice of law may be protected by consumer protection legislation in the country of your customer. For instance, the Unfair Terms and Consumer Contracts Regulations 1994 specify that they shall apply notwithstanding any contract term which applies or purports to apply the law of a non-member state, if the contract has a close connection with the territory of the member states. The Contracts (Applicable Law) Act 1990 provides that a choice of law clause shall not, in some circumstances, deprive a consumer of the protection of the mandatory rules of his country of habitual residence. 'Mandatory rules' are those which cannot be derogated from by contracts. (An example of such a clause is provided at p. 67.)

Does location of the web server determine which law applies?

A company's 'place of business' is relevant both under common laws of jurisdiction and for determining applicable law under the Rome Convention. The question whether having a web server in a country amounts to having 'a place of business' there has not been determined by the English courts. There may be a 'place of business' if the 'relevant' place has been operational for a sufficient period and some activity is carried on. A server might be seen to fulfil these criteria, particularly if it is processing contracts. However, given the nature of the web, the location of a company's server can be entirely unconnected with the locations in which its business is done. Treating companies with web servers in England as having a place of business for jurisdictional and choice of law purposes may encourage some less scrupulous traders to relocate their server to less regulated jurisdictions in an attempt to escape liabilities.

It can be seen that the question of governing law is vexed. The Rome Convention provides that a choice of law clause in an international contract will generally be respected. Thus, the prudent approach is, despite the potential pitfalls, to include a clause specifying that English law will govern the terms of your electronic contracts.

3.6 ELECTRONIC TERMS AND CONDITIONS

3.6.1 Background

What are the factors to be weighed when examining the content of a contract?

Under English law, although it may be clear that a valid contract has been made, it will still be necessary to determine the extent of the obligations that it creates. Its map must be drawn, its features delineated and its boundaries ascertained. The terms the parties have expressly included in their contract must be discovered.

The contents of the contract are not necessarily confined to those that appear on its face. The parties may have negotiated against a background of commercial or local usage whose implications they have assumed.

There are other extreme factors which affect the content of the contract in law. Additional consequences may have been annexed by statute to particular contracts. These will operate despite the party's ignorance and will prevail despite the party's contrary intention. Finally, the courts may read into the contract some further term which alone makes it effective and which the parties must be taken to have omitted by pure inadvertence. All of these implications, customary, statutory or judicial, may be as important as the terms expressly adopted by the parties.

Once the terms have been established, it does not follow that they are all of equal importance. The parties may accept that one undertaking may be regarded as of major importance. Were it to be breached, the injured party would be entitled to end the contract. Conversely, the breach of another, though demanding compensation, may leave the contract intact. Thus, in any contract rules of valuation have to be elaborated.

The courts recognise this inequality and since the end of the nineteenth century have developed a more uniform terminology to distinguish two degrees of importance. The more important terms are referred to as 'conditions', the less important as 'warranties'. Breach of a condition entitles the victim to the right to treat the contract as repudiated. The aggrieved party is not, however, bound to treat the contract as repudiated; it may instead confirm the contract. In either event, he may claim damages. Breach of warranty, on the other hand, does not entitle the victim to treat the contract as repudiated, but only to claim damages.

3.6.2 Incorporating terms and conditions

Why is it necessary to incorporate terms and conditions into a contract?

It is in the nature of things that misunderstandings and change of circumstances or, on occasion, bad faith will operate to jeopardise what the parties to a contract otherwise may consider settled. The purpose of including terms and conditions into any contract is to attempt to ensure certainty in a myriad of circumstances which typically might strain the original understanding. Should dispute arise the courts will look to and, except in extraordinary circumstances, uphold those terms to determine the rights of the parties.

It has long been settled law that terms and conditions must be made known to the parties before they enter into an agreement.

Do such requirements apply to our Internet contracts?

Yes. Contracts struck on the Internet or by e-mail are no exception. The user must be given the opportunity to read and agree to the terms and conditions. If e-mail is a chosen method of communication the incorporation of terms and conditions is straightforward. The position is more complex in relation to the World Wide Web.

The most effective notice is where your customer is required to read through your terms and conditions and signify their acceptance of those terms before proceeding. This might be achieved by using the 'scroll down and click' dialogue boxes which are increasingly used in shareware online licence agreements.

Terms which limit or exclude liabilities should in particular be clearly highlighted – use of red text with a red hand pointing to it is an effective method which some companies adopt.

3.6.3 The use of electronic terms and conditions

The Internet is revolutionary in what it makes possible in terms of free trade between businesses large and small and nation to nation. It is nonetheless merely an enabling medium. It brings together potential buyers and sellers of goods. The relations between these parties must still be regulated as with any contractual arrangement and thus it is necessary to incorporate terms and conditions into your online contract.

It is in the nature of the Internet, and indeed its principle attraction, that ease of use of desired information sets its apart from other forms of communication. Therefore, most online contracts will not be formed after lengthy discussions and negotiations over specific terms and clauses. Typically, they will be standard form contracts. Aside from key issues, such as price and type and quantity of goods or services, the terms in your online contract are not negotiated. The standard terms and conditions will usually be pre-drafted by you as Internet seller to protect your interests and the customer will only receive them at the time of purchase, usually without scrutiny.

The terms and conditions in your electronic contract often deal with more supplemental matters such as method of payment, exclusion of liability, warranties and choice of legal jurisdictions.

It is therefore essential that you understand the significance of including terms and conditions into your electronic contract with your customers or clients. Use of the Internet will require you to place greater emphasis on new or different clauses in your company's usual terms of business, in particular questions of method of contract formation, limitation of liability, warranties and choice of law.

As a vendor, your company will usually wish to include its own terms and conditions in the contract. The approach taken by many Internet traders is the 'click wrap' arrangement. This requires your potential purchaser to scroll through terms in your website before clicking on an 'accept' document. The United States courts have already upheld the validity of such an arrangement.

3.6.4 General issues to consider

What are the issues my organisation should consider when contemplating electronic terms and conditions?

The following are some of the issues which should be examined.

- *Contract formation.* Your contract terms should state the method and procedure for accepting the offer and the duration of, and conditions relating to, the offer.

- *Delivery.* The method and timing of delivery of your goods should be clarified, and in addition whether these vary depending upon method of payment, availability of your stock or the jurisdiction of your customer.

- *Risk and insurance.* Where your organisation is to despatch physical goods, the question of risk of damage or loss and the responsibility for insurance should be stated.

- *Price, currency and payment.* Your electronic contract should state the price, including any applicable taxes and insurance, and the current fee and acceptable means of payment. Where payment is to be made by physical means, such as the sending of a money order, you will doubtless wish to have the right to delay delivery until payment is received.

- *Geographical limitations.* Where your goods or services are available only in certain countries or advice can only be given in or in respect of certain jurisdictions this should be stated. Permitting third parties to post material onto your website may in itself give rise to liability. Your organisation might be responsible for any such material that contains defamatory or otherwise illegal matters. Clear terms and conditions of access and use should be displayed. Open forum discussion areas pose particular risks of libel for you as site owner. In this instance, you should consider whether discussions via e-mail would be preferable.

It is important to state at this point that the majority of the terms and conditions which your company will include in its website will relate specifically to the particular products or services you provide online. There will undoubtedly be numerous terms which you have incorporated for many years which reflect your business practice. The following specimen clauses are those additional provisions which might typically appear in a website.

3.6.5 Example clauses[6]

There are two elements to your online terms and conditions displayed on your company's website. The first is those provisions which you should include on the home page of your site. These are the 'terms of use' which govern the visitor's access and use of the website. These provisions should be prominent on the homepage, and will apply even if the visitor to the site does not ultimately purchase from your site. These terms will be split from the principle terms and conditions of sale which will appear at another location on the site, usually just before the purchaser places their online order. These terms and conditions of sale are thus the second element to your Internet standard terms and conditions.

Give me examples of some of the terms of use my company should consider adopting on our website?

Notice on home page

As we have seen (see section 3.6.2 above) for the courts to uphold any contractual terms and conditions they must be shown to have been brought to the attention of the other party before the contract was entered into. This could be effected by the use of the following suggested clause which would appear as the first paragraph in your electronic terms.

> *By using the company website ('the Site') you agree to be bound by the terms of use and, if you purchase goods using the site, you agree to be bound by the terms and conditions of sale.*

It would be advisable also to incorporate this notice on any online order form which your company posts on its website.

Terms of use

Your organisation must control the basis upon which visitors to its website use the information displayed there. This might be achieved by the following provision:

> *This Agreement by which you agree to abide in exploring and accessing information from this Site governs the terms on which you ('the User') are granted access to the Site by the 'Company'. The Site contains proprietary notices and copyright information, the terms of which the User agrees to observe and follow.*

Viruses, worms, trojan horses and other potentially destructive programs

The Internet medium is computer based and as such is prone to the associated risks of computer use. By the process of allowing visitors to access your company website and order goods or services they will be exposed to those risks while online. There is therefore a need to exclude liability so that should the visitor's system become corrupted by a virus or other destructive program which might be visited upon their system through no fault of your organisation, liability will not attach. This legal restriction could be secured by the use of a clause along the following lines:

> *The User assumes full responsibility for the protection of his computer system including computer hardware and software, stored data on his computer system and the stored data and computer systems including hardware and software of third parties who may access or be otherwise connected to the User's computer system. The User assumes the responsibility of ensuring that programs or other data downloaded or otherwise received from the Site are free from viruses, worms, trojan horses or other items of a destructive nature.*

Data security

In Chapter 9 we will examine the issue of data protection as it applies to online commerce. Your organisation must address this important consideration. However, the openness of the Internet may result in inadvertent disclosure of data. An appropriate disclaimer for such disclosure might be as follows:

> *The Company (i.e. your business) will take reasonable steps to ensure that data transmitted electronically to the Company via the Site or otherwise and stored by the Company is not accessed by unauthorised third parties. The User accepts the risk that data transmitted electronically to the Company via the Site or otherwise may be intercepted before reaching the Company or accessed from the Company's data storage means by third parties unauthorised by the Company and may be exploited unlawfully by the said unauthorised third parties. The Company does not assume responsibility for guarding against the acts of the said unauthorised third party.*

Connected sites

In sections 2.6 and 6.2 we consider the law which governs linking to other websites and the risk of, for example, defamation by such means. It is therefore important for your company to protect itself in this sphere. A typical clause which accomplishes that might be as follows:

> *The Company makes no representations as to the security or propriety of any website which may be accessed through the site. Connected websites accessed through the Site are independent websites over which the Company does not exercise any control, whether financial, editorial or of other kind, and are not in any way endorsed by the Company.*

Information contained in the site

If you are using your organisation's website to conduct sales then of necessity you will be compelled to provide information about your business and its product or services. It is essential that you appreciate the need to show the utmost good faith and accuracy when so detailing. Indeed, no attempt at restriction will obviate the impact of UK legislation governing misdescription. Nonetheless, the information on your site might well be subject to change at your instance for cogent reasons and in the final analysis should only be for guidance and assistance to visitors. To make clear its purpose you should consider including the following clause:

> *Information contained in the Site may contain technical inaccuracies or typographical mistakes. Information may be changed or updated without notice and any queries relating to the information including queries as to its recency or accuracy should be addressed to: [   ].*
>
> *All information made available from within this website is provided 'as is' for information purposes only and without warranty of any kind, either express or implied, including but not limited to any warranties as to non-infringement costs, merchantability or fitness for a particular purpose.*

Exclusion of liability

In section 3.4 we considered the question of attempts by companies to limit or exclude liability in certain situations. As stated, exemption clauses may be a perfectly legitimate device in contracts between parties of equal bargaining power. In the context of online transactions they also have a proper place. Your company may wish to restrict or exclude liability in a variety of circumstances, but such attempts must not fall foul of statutory restrictions (see section 3.4). A more generic clause your business might apply is as follows:

In no circumstances will the Company be liable for the use of any direct or indirect, consequential, special or other damage howsoever resulting from the use of this Site or any other website connected to the Site by means of a hypertext link or otherwise (whether such damage is caused by transmission from the site or a connected website to the User's computer system of viruses, worms, trojan horses or other destructive items, corrupted data or data incompatible with the User's computer system or third party's interception of or access to data of whatever nature including without limitation personal data and credit and payment card information transmitted by the User electronically to the Company or otherwise howsoever caused, such damage to include, without limitation, lost profits, interruption to business, loss on the whole or any part of a program or programs or any data howsoever stored whether saved on a computer system or otherwise.

General

As your organisation embraces Internet trading, it will face the inevitable tension between the desire to ensure that all relevant contractual terms are incorporated into its electronic contract and the limitation of screen size and the need to use the new medium effectively. In respect of your electronic contract, you will need to consider, as with any contract, the appropriate extent and content of your contractual terms.

We have considered above the significance of using online terms and conditions. Let us now examine some of the more salient provisions which your organisation may wish to adopt in its website to govern the trading relationship with its customers or clients.

Your company will doubtless have its own standard terms and conditions of sale. The specimen clauses which appear here are only intended to draw your attention to those provisions which will not be incorporated in your terms simply because those terms were not written for online application. It will therefore be necessary for you to include many additional terms and the purpose of the following general provision is to make clear that visitors will take subject to all your sale conditions as displayed on your website:

Unless expressly otherwise stated in respect of a particular sale made on or through the site, all sale agreements between the 'Company' and the 'Purchaser' effected on or through the site will be in accordance with and subject to the following terms and conditions: ...

The company may at any time, in its sole discretion and without prior notice, change these terms and conditions.

Terms and conditions of sale

The second element to your online terms are your terms and conditions of sale. These must be sufficiently brought to the attention of your online customer before they enter into the contract. Most sites thus require the visitor to go through a pre-programmed page on the site which requires the user to click on an 'accept' button to signify consent. This process prevents a purchaser denying they had sight of your electronic terms and conditions when they entered into the contract. When your website is being developed it is important you make clear to the website developer that you require the site to be programmed in this way.

Can you give us some examples of clauses we might include in our Internet terms and conditions?

Acceptance of order

In section 3.1 above we referred to the need for acceptance of an offer in law and in particular at what moment acceptance is deemed to have taken place. The purpose of the following clause is to set out with certainty how this is to be achieved:

> *All orders must be made on the standard order form contained in the purchasing section of this Site. An order is not binding on the Company until the order form is received at the Company's order processing department. When the order processing department receives a properly completed order form, a notification will be send electronically to the purchaser.*

Intellectual property

In Chapter 7 we consider the issue of your company's intellectual property rights. It is necessary for you to control the use of those rights and this can be achieved by the use of an appropriate clause in your website terms and conditions. The following is an example of such a provision:

> *The goods sold are for use within the United Kingdom. The Company will not accept liability of any kind for infringement or alleged infringements of foreign, that is to subsisting outside the United Kingdom, patents, trade marks, copyrights, design rights and other intellectual property rights arising out of the Purchaser's profession, distribution, use offer or exposure or sale outside the United Kingdom of goods purchased under this Agreement.*

> *The Purchaser agrees to indemnify the Company against all or any claims for infringement of foreign patents, copyrights, trade marks, design rights or other intellectual property rights arising out of the Purchaser's possession, distribution, use, offer or exposure for sale or sale of goods purchased under this Agreement.*

Delivery charges and title to the goods

If your organisation is supplying goods which are required to be delivered then the question of the attendent cost and title is important. The following is an example of how this issue might be addressed:

> *The goods will be deemed delivered to the Purchaser on despatch from the company's warehouse/factory and title to the goods will pass on such delivery. The Purchaser from delivery will be responsible for all charges in relation to the goods including without limitation local and national taxes, freight or shipping charges, handling charges or other similar expenses. If the Company incurs any such taxes or charges on behalf of the Purchaser in relation to the goods, then the Purchaser shall within 14 days of being notified of the incurring of the said charges or taxes reimburse the same.*

Product specification

Your company will no doubt be constantly altering its products and if those products are being made available on the Internet then you will want to provide for such alteration. This might be accomplished by the following:

> *All goods sold are of the specifications listed in this website. The Company reserves the right to make modifications to the specification of any of its goods or, in the event of chosen goods not being available, to supply substitute goods provided that such modifications do not materially alter the performance of the goods or the purpose or purposes for which they can be used or that such substitute goods are the specification equivalent to or better than the specification of the goods ordered.*

Governing law

In section 3.5 we examined the vital significance of controlling the legal jurisdiction of any contractual arrangement entered into online. The following is an example of an appropriate provision:

If not actually the case, the contract under which you use the website shall be deemed to have been made in England and the construction, validity and performance of these terms and conditions shall be governed in all respects by English law and the English courts shall have non-exclusive jurisdiction in respect of any dispute between you and the Company concerning your use of this website.

CHECKLIST: HOW TO FORM AN ELECTRONIC CONTRACT

- Does your website incorporate a notice specifying the visitors' terms of use of the site?

- Have you notified your website developer that your website must be programmed to ensure your terms and conditions be passed through prior to your online customer placing an order?

- Do your electronic terms and conditions make clear the distinction between offer and invitation to treat and do they provide absolute clarity on how acceptance is communicated?

- Do your terms and conditions include provisions relating to protection of your intellectual property rights, delivery of products and specifications?

- Does your website publish a privacy policy complying with vigorous data protection requirements?

- Check that your company's business processes are properly aligned with your e-commerce activities and that your electronic terms and conditions reflect this.

NOTES

1. *Spencer* v. *Harding* (1870).
2. *Pharmaceutical Society of Great Britain* v. *Boots Cash Chemists (Southern) Limited* [1953] 1 All ER 482; [1953] 2 WLR 427; [1953] 1 QB 394, CA.
3. *Fisher* v. *Bell* [1961] 1 QB 394.
4. *Partridge* v. *Crittenden* [1968] 2 All ER 421, DC.
5. The Court of Appeal decided after many years of uncertainty that there is such a category as a unilateral contract in *United Dominions Trust (Commercial) Limited* v. *Eagle Aircraft Services Limited* [1968] 1 All ER 104; [1968] 1 WLR 74; [1968] 111 SJ 849, CA.

6. The clauses set out in this section are intended as guidance only to some of the issues to be considered for online contracts. They are not to be treated as precedents appropriate to all types of business. The reader is advised to seek full legal advice on the proper use of online terms and conditions.

How to make and accept payment over the Internet

4.1 INTRODUCTION

As the potential for the Internet to serve as an instrument of commerce has assumed clarity, the inevitable vexed issue of how one can make payment online has developed with equal temper.

The majority of transactions made over the Internet at present use existing payment products such as credit card numbers, sometimes in conjunction with encryption. For electronic commerce to thrive, new and easier forms of electronic payment will be necessary.

The primary concern has always been one of security. Most electronic mail messages are usually sent unencrypted. That is to say, anyone who incepts an electronic mail message could read its contents without difficulty. This has resulted in an understandable reluctance by users to send their credit card details in an e-mail message that could be read by any other user.

In everyday life there are three ways of paying for goods or services. One can pay in cash, write a cheque or use a credit card. The same mechanisms are becoming available to online merchants. A credit card number can be encrypted (see below) and the order processed manually. Alternatively, a credit card order can be processed electronically. One can always send cash having placed an order on the Internet.

In this chapter we will consider the interaction of the Internet and the laws of money. In addition, the various payment systems which are designed to address this concern and the range of regulatory standards which impact upon payment systems will be examined.

The UK government believes that a lack of universally agreed standards for electronic money products may act as an damper on their development as alternative payment methods. Moreover, any regulation must be proportionate to the risks presented. Disproportionate or badly targeted regulation in the early stages of electronic money schemes could discourage their further development. Premature or incomplete regulation could distort the market or only catch certain variations of electronic money.[1]

In order to consider the possibilities of payment systems associated with electronic commerce we should first examine the essential elements of a more traditional payment process.

4.2 TRADITIONAL PAYMENT PROCESS: THE CHEQUE

A cheque is a form of bill of exchange.

What is a bill of exchange?

A bill of exchange is defined as:

> *An unconditional order in writing, addressed by one person to another, signed by the person giving it, requiring the person to whom it is addressed to pay on demand or at a fixed or determinable future time a sum certain in money to or to the order of a specified person, or to the bearer.*[2]

A cheque is defined as a bill of exchange drawn on a banker payable on demand.[3]

For the necessary ingredients of these long-established payment methods to have any application to the Internet they must be capable of being transferred to the online environment. Each of the features of a bill of exchange can be so transferred to an electronic form by the use of cryptography.

4.3 ELECTRONIC PAYMENT SYSTEMS

In this section, we will examine some forms of electronic payment systems together with ordinary credit card use. The issues which cause concern with regard to payment on the Internet are broadly similar to those which pertain whenever a new method of payment has been developed.

What are the primary concerns relating to electronic payment?

The security of the transaction between payer and payee. The identity of the payer and irrevocability of the payment are also factors. Universal acceptance of the type of electronic payment is something which causes an inertia to the acceptance of payment online.

The fact that electronic payments involve electronic transfers is of course not unique. Most retailers employ debit card transactions which are also electronic transactions.

4.3.1 Credit cards

At the present time most business-to-consumer (B2C) transactions conducted online are effected by credit card payments. The purchaser inserts their credit card details by completing an online form which is then transmitted to the seller over the Internet. The transmission is usually encrypted (see section 6.3 below) which provides additional security.

What is the attraction of using credit cards?

From the consumer's point of view, credit cards are familiar. They need not enter into additional agreements and there are no currency conversion problems. Moreover, the consumer buying online using their credit card has the protection of the Consumer Credit Act 1974, placing them in a better position than if paying by cash.

What is the protection afforded by the Consumer Credit Act 1974?

Section 75 of the Act applies to transactions where any single item is worth between £100 and £30 000. If there is no pre-existing agreement between the card issuer and the supplier, the cardholder has enhanced legal rights. They can pursue either the supplier or the card issuer itself for misrepresentation or breach of contract. This is because the Act makes the card supplier jointly and severally liable. From your point of view, as a business selling goods or services, using credit cards also has advantages. There is no need for specialist equipment to be installed by your potential customer and thus shopping online is easier for Internet purchasers.

The principal disadvantages to you as a vendor is the need for you to enter into a merchant account with a card issuer. This is necessary to allow you to accept credit cards. Transaction costs are also a factor to be considered.

How will online credit card sales be treated?

Internet card payment transactions are classed as card not present ('CNP') transactions. As the cardholder (and the card) is not physically with you at the time of the transaction, it is not possible for you to check the card details or the customer's signature.

There are risks associated with CNP transactions which your organisation must understand and make a commercial judgment upon. Whenever you undertake an Internet transaction, there is no guarantee of payment. If your online customer should query the transaction at a later date or any discrepancies arise the card issuer may resort to a charge back to recover funds from you. In modern commerce, there are an increasing number of transactions which take place every day where the cardholder is not present at the point of sale. Regrettably, fraud is common where the cardholder is not present.

What might our online customers who use credit cards say?

They may claim that the card was used fraudulently or deny the transaction. They might maintain that the card has been stolen or claim that the card number has been used without their authority. Finally, they may say that they never received your goods or argue that your goods were defective, not as described or not of merchantable quality.

All of the above can result in a charge back. It is thus in your organisation's interests to encourage your staff to record details accurately and to be vigilant.

What prudent steps should we take?

Your company should always keep a record of the details of the transaction. This is because you may need to provide your credit card merchant with them if your customer queries the transaction with their card company at a later date. Your filing system should allow you to recover information easily, by date of transaction or your customer's card number. Records should be retained for at least three years.

How does the legal relationship between us as Internet vendor, the card issuer and our online customer work?

The 1987 case of Recharge Card Services[4] established that using a credit card creates three distinct legal contracts. The first is the contract of supply between your company and your card-holding online customer. Second is the contract between your company and the card-issuing company. The card issuer undertakes to honour the card by paying you on presentation of the sales voucher. Thirdly, there is the contract between the card-issuing company and your Internet customer. Here, your card-holding customer undertakes to reimburse the card issuer for all payments made or liabilities incurred by the card issuer to you as a result of your customer's use of their credit card. It can be seen that in each contract, each party is involved in two of the three contracts but none is party to all three.

What is the effect of the relationship between the three contracts?

A card holder who purchases by credit card completes his contract with your company as supplier. Your company must then look to the card issuer for payment. The effect is that, if the card issuer fails to pay you – for example, if the issuer becomes insolvent – you cannot then seek payment from your online customer.

What other risk might my organisation face if we adopt credit cards as a means of our customers buying online?

The most significant risk is one which pertains to any retailer who subscribes to a credit card merchant agreement. Section 83 of the Consumer Credit Act 1974 states that generally a consumer cannot be made liable for the misuse of his credit card by a third party. Usually, the credit card agreement makes the card holder liable for the first £50 while the card is not in their possession until the card issuer receives notification of the card's loss.

Nonetheless, your online credit card customer can, within a certain time limit, dispute a transaction that may be the result of theft, fraud or error. If the card issuer accepts that payment should not proceed a 'charge back' occurs. Your company may not only have to repay the disputed sums but also a processing fee. Given that frequently your online customers may only make very modest value purchases on any one transaction the processing fee might exceed the transaction value.

Why is the risk of charge backs higher if selling on the Internet?

Simply because you will not be physically face to face with your customer. If you were, you can verify the customer's signature against the signature on the back of the card. The payment is therefore treated as a 'card holder not present' transaction.

Why is the increased risk of charge backs a potential problem for us?

As all transactions which you complete online will be conducted in this way, it might prove more difficult for your company to obtain a merchant account. It will usually require your company to provide additional eligibility information. Thus your business may have to disclose its volume of business, credit history, cost of goods, debt load, length of time in business and refund policies to the card issuer.

Another factor you should consider is this. If your goods or services can actually be delivered electronically they can be denied more easily. Where physical goods are supplied, you, as seller, can usually prove that the goods have been delivered to your credit and customer's address. The customer cannot therefore argue that the transaction did not take place. They can only allege that the goods were not what they ordered or were defective. If you are delivering online, while the cost of reproducing and delivering your goods might be lower, you may suffer the payment of numerous charge backs with attendant processing fees. If this were multiplied, your company might even lose its merchant account.

4.3.2 Secure electronic transactions (SET)

Hitherto encryption methods (see section 6.3 below) used 'private systems'. This required both sender and receiver to use and hold a copy of the same encryption key. The problem was that a third party who obtained access to the key could also read any messages which they intercepted. To combat this flaw 'public key cryptography' was developed. The 'secure electronic payment protocol' is based on this technology. Its aim was to provide an agreed security standard for use in making payments over the Internet.

Why was the secure electronic payment protocol established?

It was intended to maintain the privacy of Internet transactions. In addition, it addressed the needs for the identity of the payer to be verified so that his or her instructions could be relied upon.

How does SET work?

Two separate keys, one public and one private, are used to encode and decode the message. The public one used encrypts the message using a complex formula. The message is then transmitted over the Internet in an encrypted form. The public key is published in a directory and therefore can be accessed by third parties. However, the message sent can only be read using the private key – and this will only be known to the receiver.

How is the identity of the sender established?

By the use of digital certificates. These verify that the individual company concerned has the authority to use the public key in which the message sent is encrypted. The certificates are in the form of small electronic documents issued by certificate authorities (see Chapter 9). The use of these certificates is coupled with the use of a digital signature which operates by encrypting the message in a cryptographic algorithm called a hash function. The encryption is made using the sender's private key. The sender's public key is then used by a recipient to reconstitute the hash and is compared with other hashes generated by the sender for authenticity. This process of authenticating identity is analogous to checking a handwritten signature on a cheque against a cheque card.

How can my company ensure non-repudiation by the sender?

A traditional payment method such as a cheque can be cancelled at any point before it is cashed. The only way to achieve irrevocability with online payment is to take one further step. It is necessary to incorporate into your electronic terms and conditions an express stipulation that any instructions/payments are irrevocable once sent unless proved to be non-authentic.

CHECKLIST: HOW TO MAKE AND ACCEPT PAYMENT OVER THE INTERNET

- Do you appreciate the attraction of offering a credit card facility online?
- Are you conversant with the associated risks of collecting payment via credit card?
- Have you a broad understanding of the other methods of electronic payment?

NOTES

1. See *Net benefits, the electronic commerce agenda for the UK*, published by the DTI.

2. Bills of Exchange Act 1882, section 3.

3. Bills of Exchange Act 1882, section 73.

5

How to authenticate contracts concluded over the Internet

5.1 INTRODUCTION

In establishing your corporate website the aim must surely be to encourage visitors. Preventing visitors must have little commercial benefit. However, visitors must be authenticated before transactions can take place.

The method of authentication used depends on the value and risk of the transaction you wish to effect. For low-value low-risk transactions, sufficient authentication is provided in the credit card details. Such a transaction is, after all, no different from your customer or client using a credit card over the telephone. However, for high-value or higher-risk transactions you may require your customers to set up an account or be financially vetted before interactive trading. In this situation, your customers or clients would be provided with a password or personal identifier, for example a PIN. If the transaction values are very high or the perceived risk is significant, for example stock trading, then digital signatures can be used for authentication.

5.2 CRYPTOGRAPHY

What is cryptography?

Cryptography is the method of disguising the contents of a message, used from ancient times to the present. In the context of the Internet cryptography is the science of keeping communications private. Cryptography has long been applied by banks and is an essential tool for electronic commerce. Cryptography can be used as the basis of an electronic signature or to keep electronic data confidential. It also ensures that the integrity of such information is preserved. A central element of cryptography is encryption. This is the transformation of data into an unintelligible form.

5.3 ENCRYPTION

Explain encryption

Encryption is the process by which a message is disguised sufficiently to hide the substance of the content.

Encryption involves turning normal text into a series of letters and/or numbers which can only be deciphered by someone who has the correct password or key. Encryption is used to prevent others reading confidential, private or commercial data (for example an e-mail sent over the Internet or a file stored on floppy disk).

In essence, contemporary cryptographic search systems change readable symbols into a second set of unreadable symbols using a mathematical process controlled by a number. This number is called a key. The following indicates the process involved:

Your Company A writes to Company B

We agree your terms.

The message is encrypted as follows:

'196421043520418N620181727227'

To read the message, Company B must know how the message was encrypted. If they know the key to the unreadable symbols, they can work out the message when they receive it. This example does not adequately demonstrate the use of the mathematical formula that may be involved but is intended to illustrate how the concept works.

There are two types of mathematical formulae that permit your message to be disguised.

5.3.1 Symmetric cryptographic systems (secret key)

As the name suggests, the same number key is used to encrypt and decrypt the message. Two people can use the same system to send and receive encrypted messages to each other. This system allows very long keys which means that the message can be very secure, because it would take an eternity for a computer to find the proper numerical key to break the code. The system's effectiveness depends on the strength of the algorithm and the length of the key number. The longer the key number, the stronger the key. Such a key is suitable for closed user groups where there is a strong element of mutual trust between your company and others in the group.

There are, however, disadvantages. The key must be kept secure and secret. Two people must have the key to communicate. If your company wishes to receive encrypted messages from a large number of people, it will have to give out a large number of keys and rely on those people with access to the key to ensure that it is kept secure and secret. Thus your company may be reluctant to permit people to obtain access to your site by means of a secret key because of the large number of keys you will have to send out. Alternatively, your company might consider this a benefit, rather analogous to supermarkets which provide loyalty cards, so your site might have private keys for customers for the same reasons. This type of key can be useful in some circumstances. A problem exists, however, in establishing the authenticity of the person that sent the message. If the message is sent by a forger, you will not be aware that the sender of the message has used the key improperly. This problem can be overcome by maintaining full records, but they represent an added evidential burden on the system.

5.3.2 Asymmetric cryptographic systems (public key)

This system involves two number keys and it can work in two ways.

Private public key

If your company wants to encrypt information, you can generate your own public and private keys using the software on your computer. Although you keep the private key numbers secret, you notify everybody that you want to know that your company has a public key number and post it on the Internet. If company B wants to write a confidential e-mail to you, they can obtain your public key number and use it to encrypt the message. Company B can comfort itself that only you can read the e-mail because only your key number will decrypt the message.

Is there a problem with private public key systems?

Yes. If an imposter wanted to disrupt your organisation by interrupting your ability to receive and send encrypted messages, they could. They could generate their own public and private keys, post the public key on the Internet and claim it belongs to you. Company B might think they are sending messages to you but in fact the message is posted to the imposter. In addition, the imposter could use his or her own private key to send messages to company B, which would assume they came from you.

Certification authorities

Certification authorities or trusted third parties are public or private bodies that act to certify the connection between a person and their public key number. The certification authority guarantees the authenticity of the public key number. The certification authority issues an 'electronic authentication certificate', which has the following characteristics:

- it identifies the certification authority;
- it identifies the subscriber;
- it contains the subscriber's public key;
- it is digitally signed with the certification authority's private key.

The electronic authentication certificate also contains other information, such as the level of enquiry carried out by the certification authority before issuing the certificate.

How does my company acquire such a certificate?

You will provide the certification authority with a copy of your public key number and proof of your identity, together with sufficient credentials to demonstrate your authority to deal with high-value transactions. When your company sends a message to company B, you also send company B a copy of your certificate. Company B's computer will decrypt the message according to the key they have been given. At the same time, the certification authority will confirm to company B that:

- you are who you purport to be;
- your certificate has not been revoked or expired.

In summary, the role of certification authorities is to provide certificates that establish the identity of the owner of the public key number.

5.4 THE ELECTRONIC COMMUNICATIONS ACT 2000

In 2000 the government introduced the Electronic Communications Act. The main purpose of the Act is to help build confidence in electronic commerce and its underlying technology, although the Act is not an all-embracing guide to the law of e-commerce. The multiple legal considerations which must be addressed if embarking upon an e-business strategy form the subject of this book. The Act is, however, a significant element of the government's policy to facilitate electronic commerce.

What does the Act provide for?

First, it provides an approval scheme for businesses and other organisations providing cryptography services, such as electronic signature services and confidentiality services (see section 5.5 below).

Second, it gives legal recognition to electronic signatures, and third it removes obstacles in other legislation to the use of electronic communication and storage in place of paper. The Act also contains provisions to update proceedings for modifying telecommunications licences.

The Act is in three parts:

- *Part I – Cryptography Service Providers*. This concerns the arrangements for registering providers of cryptography support services, such as electronic signature services and confidentiality services.
- *Part II – Facilitation of Electronic Commerce, Data Storage, etc.* This part of the Act makes provision for the legal recognition of electronic signatures. It will also facilitate the use of electronic communications or electronic storage of information as an alternative to traditional means of communication or storage.
- *Part III – Miscellaneous and Supplemental*. This part of the legislation is concerned with the modification of telecommunication licences and, *inter alia*, territorial extent of the Act.

For the purposes of this book we shall consider Parts I and II of the Act.

5.4.1 Part I – Cryptography Service Providers

How does the Act regulate this service?

The Act creates a register of approved providers. Section 1 places a duty on the Secretary of State to establish and maintain a register of approved providers of cryptography support services, and specifies what information is contained in the register. The public have right of access to the register and any changes to it must be publicised.

The idea behind the register is that it will be voluntary but will promote minimum standards of quality and service to be met in relation to cryptography support services. The government has indicated that, if the self-regulatory scheme works, there will be no need to set up a statutory scheme. The provisions in the Act relating to the establishment of the statutory scheme are subject to a 'sunset clause'. This states that if a statutory scheme has not been set up within five years then the government's power to set one up will lapse.

What are cryptography support services?

Cryptography support services include:

- ensuring confidentiality, that is ensuring that electronic communications or data can be accessed or put into an intelligible form, that is restored to the condition in which it was before any encryption or similar process was applied to it, only by certain persons;
- ensuring that the authenticity or integrity of electronic communications or data is capable of being ascertained. This is achieved by the use of an electronic signature (see section 5.5 below).

The Act makes clear that the approval scheme for cryptography support services only includes those services primarily involved in a continuing relationship between the supplier of the service and your customer. Cryptography support services include registration and certification in relation to certificates (see section 5.3.2 above), time stamping of certificates or documents, key generation and management, key storage and providing directories of certificates.

5.4.2 Part II – Facilitation of Electronic Commerce, Data Storage, etc.

The Act provides for the admissibility of electronic signatures and related certificates in legal proceedings. (For a full examination of digital signatures see section 5.5 below.)

Who will be the arbiter of whether an electronic signature has been correctly used?

The courts will decide on this question of authentication or integrity of a message in the event of dispute.

Is it possible for my company to contract with another business on how our respective electronic signatures are to be treated?

Yes, the Act does not cast doubt on such an arrangement.

Can an electronic signature be used as evidence of authenticity or integrity in court proceedings?

Yes, section 7(1) allows an electronic signature or its certification to be admissible as evidence on this question.

What is meant by authenticity of an electronic communication?

First, whether the communication or data comes from a particular person or other source. Second, whether it is accurately timed and dated. Finally, whether it is intended to have legal effect.

What do references to 'integrity' mean?

This is where there has been any tampering with or other modification of the communication or data.

What is the impact of the Act upon other legislation?

One concern raised during the government's consultation period highlights this issue. The outdated definitions of words such as 'writing' and 'signature' in law are potentially significant barriers to the development of electronic commerce in this country. However, there is a clear need for swift legislative action in the area of electronic commerce generally. The Electronic Communications Act 2000 is the first available legislative opportunity to address the dawn of e-commerce. The Act does, however, include a power in clause 8 to enable ministers to draw up secondary legislation to permit such requirements to be met electronically. For example, the DTI plans to use powers under the Act to amend the Companies Act 1985 to enable companies to communicate with shareholders electronically. However, there may be a few examples where it is not appropriate to take such a step, at least in the near future. The publication of an analysis of the references in the legislation to 'in writing' or 'signed' was not compatible with the timetable of bringing the Act before Parliament. The Society for Computers and Law have estimated that there may be as many as 40 000 references to 'writing' and signature in current legislation alone.

5.5 DIGITAL SIGNATURES

5.5.1 Background

In this work there is frequent reference to the concern which exists in connection with the safety of using the Internet for trading purposes. That concern, while largely misplaced, is perhaps founded on a natural reservation to proceed when faced with a new medium. Two areas where concern is manifest are the issues of authentication and electronic signatures. Traditionally, both business practice and the law have required commercial agreements to be evidenced. The reasons for this are certainty and accountability and this necessarily applies with equal force to electronic commerce.

The widespread deployment and use of electronic commerce will be determined by the trust and confidence users of the Internet have in the technology and the organisation providing the services. The deployment of public key cryptography or electronic signatures helps to both guarantee the integrity of information and link the information to a person, thereby preventing repudiation. An adequate legal framework for electronic signatures is widely regarded as an essential factor in the development of electronic commerce. In this section we will examine the important factor of authentication. The issue of how to authenticate an online contract under English law is not straightforward. While the technical basis of a digital signature is not the preserve of this book, in this section we will touch upon the legal constraints which a new recognised electronic signature system must operate within.

To some extent the solutions to the problem of ensuring certainty can be gleaned from the application of existing law to electronic commerce. However, it is clear from relevant legislative activity throughout EU member states that existing laws do not satisfactorily deal with electronic signatures. It is here that the problem's infancy may actually allow a level of legal uniformity as countries can approach the question without historical ties. As the issue is new, standardisation of legal treatment could be a realistic possibility.

What is a digital or electronic signature?

A digital or electronic signature verifies the contents of a message and the identity of the signatory. It is the equivalent of a manual signature. However, it is in no way a manipulation of a handwritten signature. It also provides a method of ensuring that a document was in fact sent by a particular sender. This feature is known as non-repudiation. A digital signature can be used to give the recipient confirmation that the communication comes from who it purports to come from (authenticity).

Another important use of the electronic signature is to establish that the communication has not been tampered with (integrity). Provided a secure cryptographic hash function is used to generate the digital signature, there is no way to extract someone's digital signature from one document and attach it to another. Neither is it possible to alter a signed message in any way. The slightest change in a signed document will cause the digital signature verification process to fail.

We shall review the question from the perspective of your organisation's trading website.

How does the secure signature process work?

Suppose your chief executive wishes to send a copy of a contract to your financial director for his comments. The chief executive passes a message through an algorithm called a 'digest' or 'hash' function. The hash carries out a mathematical operation on the original message. It creates a unique and precise version of the original text. This is called the 'message digest'. Any change in the message, no matter how slight, will cause significant changes in the message itself. The message digest is very short in comparison to the actual message, so it does not take long to carry out this function. Your finance director then encrypts the message digest with his private key. This encryption forms the actual digital signature of the message. The digital signature is a message digest and the private key. The chief executive can send the plain text with the digital signature or, he can keep the details of the contract confidential by encrypting the message using the finance director's public key. When the finance director receives a message, his computer and software perform separate operations to identify the identity of the sender and to determine whether the message was altered in transit. To verify the chief executive's identity the finance director's system takes the chief executive's digital signature and uses his public key to decrypt the digital signature. This will produce a message digest. If successful, the finance director can be sure that the chief executive sent the message because he is the only person with access to his private key.

Are digital signatures fallible?

Yes. Suppose, for example, your chairman, with whom your chief executive is negotiating takes the chief executive's private key away from him at the meeting they are attending. The chairman then sends a message to the finance director, asking for a quick reply because of the sensitivity of the contract. In this instance, the finance director has not established the identity of the sender, despite the technology used.

How does English law define digital signatures?

Section 7(2) of the Electronic Communications Act 2000 defines digital signatures as:

> *Anything in electronic form as ... is incorporated into or otherwise logically associated with any electronic communication or electronic data and purports to be so incorporated or associated for the purpose of being used in establishing the authenticity of the communication as data in the integrity of the communication or data, or both.*

What is the technical basis for a digital signature?

An electronic or digital signature is based on the application to electronic data of an algorithm contained within the data stream which authenticates the identity of the sender. This is achieved by encoding the document until the intended recipient unlocks the data stream. The process relies on the technology of cryptography (see sections 5.2 and 5.3 above). Public and private key cryptography allows individuals to sign electronic documents. A message which has been encrypted with your company's 'private key' can be decrypted with the 'public key' from that key pair.

If one applies the public key to a message or document which has been encrypted with any key other than the 'private key' of that particular company or individual it will produce scrambled data. To signify a consent to the terms of the document online, one can 'sign' it by adding a statement of acceptance to it and then encrypting it by applying one's private key. This encrypted version is thus capable of being treated as a signed contract as it could only have been encrypted by using the signer's private key.

What is the function of an electronic or digital signature?

It is intended to fix the certainty of contracting parties and acceptance of the terms of agreement between them. This is an essential part of contracting over the Internet.

One of the advantages a digital signature has over a physical signature is the ability to 'time' stamp the signature. The date may be added after a physical signature has been endorsed on a contract. The signature of itself cannot evidence the time at which agreement of contractual terms was reached. However, this can be achieved by the application of a digital signature.

For a digital signature to satisfy a standard of certainty acceptable in terms of law it must adhere to the following requirements:

- should be unique in that it can only be created by the user;
- it must be impossible to forge;
- authentication ought to be easy;
- it should be impossible to deny – the author of a digital signature should not be able to deny true authorship.

How can we verify the identity of the digital signatory?

There exists two methods of authentication: first, authentication directly by the recipient, and second, authentication by third parties who act as arbiters – indirect signature authentication.

From a legal perspective, with the law's necessary emphasis on evidence, authentication by a third party is clearly preferable. The third party could keep the public data generated by senders and used by receivers to validate signatures. Your organisation can incorporate a 'trusted third party' as part of its digital signature. That third party will act as arbiter in the event of a dispute between your business and your customer.

Are there any other problems with digital signature?

The simple use of digital signatures does not of itself remove legal difficulties relating to the question of authentication. Conducting business using electronic signatures requires a different mindset to conventional contract management because there are different risks. For example, when an electronic signature is incorporated into a document, it has the effect of finding every single part of it and links the authority of the signor with every single comma and colon. It is much more than signing the end of the document and initialling every page.

5.6 FORGERY

Forgery of one's signature is a risk, albeit modest, which all of us face in everyday life and in business. The forging of paper documents in itself rarely brings any advantage to the forger. The forgery is usually done as a prior step to the commission of some other crime, most often a crime of deception, which will result in some material advantage (most obviously money or other property) to the forger. Forgery and counterfeiting are regulated by the Forgery and Counterfeiting Act 1981. It is useful at this point to consider the criminal offence of forgery as it exists in English law. Such a review sets the examination of the risks and liabilities associated with digital signatures in context.

What is the definition of forgery?

A person is guilty of forgery if he makes a false instrument and for this purpose 'instrument' is defined by section 8 of the Act:

> ... 'instrument' means that
>
> (a) ... any document, whether of a formal or informal character;
>
> (b) ... any disk, tape, soundtrack or other device on or in which information is recorded or stored by mechanical, electronic or other means.

It can be seen that the Internet can constitute an 'instrument' for the purposes of the statutory definition.

Section 9 of the Act states:

> (i) an instrument is false for the purpose of this part of this Act:
>
>   (a) if it purports to have been saved in the form in which it is made by a person who did not in fact make it in that form; or
>
>   (b) if it purports to have been made in the form in which it is on the authority of a person who did not in fact authorise its making in that form; or
>
>   (c) if it purports to have been made in the terms in which it is made by the person who did not in fact make it in those terms; or

> *(d)* *if it purports to have been made in the terms in which it is made on the authority of a person who did not in fact authorise its making in those terms; or ....*
>
> *(h)* *if it purports to have been made or altered by an existing person but he did not in fact exist.*
>
> *(ii)* *a person is to be treated ... as making a false instrument if he alters an instrument so as to make it false in any respect ...*

How might fraudulent activity find a home with digital signatures?

A digital signature on the Internet, unlike a physical signature, does not come from a human hand but from an artefact. Unauthorised access to this artefact can lead to the production of signed contractual documents and payment orders which are the same as the genuine articles.

Is there any guidance as to how the English courts will treat the problem of a fraudulently issued digital signature?

There has at the time of writing been one case concerning reliance on a fraudulently issued electronic signature. The case is *Standard Bank London Limited* v. *The Bank of Tokyo Limited.*[1]

The case concerned a 'tested telex'. This is a telex authenticated by a secret code known only to the sender and the recipient. The recipient's bank relied upon the tested telex received from the sending bank as confirming the authenticity of a documentary letter of credit. The document of credit was forged. The forgers had reproduced an issue of the tested telex by the sending bank. The court held that the recipient of the tested telex would be able to rely on it unless the recipient:

- was on notice of dishonesty; or

- was aware of facts that should have put it on enquiry as to dishonesty; or

- had been wilfully blind.

The sending bank was liable for the loss suffered by the recipient bank.

What was the rationale for the court's decision?

The decision was in the context of evidence that the banking system relies on tested telexes and that they are intended to avoid arguments about authority.

What is the legal effect of the Standard Bank decision?

The decision places the responsibility for keeping keys secure fairly and squarely on the person using the key to authenticate a message. It absolves you as recipient from any duty to enquire into the authenticity of the method unless you are on notice of dishonesty. The practical effect is to give senders an incentive to take security precautions.

Control of such abuse in its simplest form would entail making the holder of the digital signature liable for all signatures generated by the artefact unless and until the keyholder has revoked the digital signature's authority.

CHECKLIST: HOW TO AUTHENTICATE CONTRACTS CONCLUDED OVER THE INTERNET

- Do you understand the principles of cryptography?
- Are you familiar with the role of certification authorities?
- Do you know what a digital signature is?
- Do you understand how a digital signature is used?
- Do you know why the Electronic Communications Act 2000 was introduced?
- Do you appreciate the significance of legal recognition of digital signatures?
- Do you understand the role of cryptography service providers?

NOTE

1. *Standard Bank London Ltd* v. *Bank of Tokyo Limited* [1997] 2 Lloyd's Reports 169, QBD.

How to manage your company's e-mail risks

6.1 THE LAW AND ELECTRONIC MAIL

As the information revolution sails on into a new century, most businesses are already being carried along by it. Access to computers is continually increasing and e-mail is rapidly becoming one of the key means of communication.

One may be routinely sending and receiving electronic mail in the course of business without necessarily using the organisation's website for the purpose of selling goods or services online. Thus the issues which follow in this section relate to the general use of e-mail within organisations. However, the examination herein is closely linked to the transmission of e-mail in so far as it relates to the purpose of transacting business on behalf of your business.

E-mail is intended to boost productivity, improve communications and cut operational costs. The user of e-mail need not be held in a telephone queue or be confronted with an electronic voicemail. It is faster than the traditional postal service and mail programs can even be set to establish exactly when messages are read.

How does e-mail work?

Electronic mail is transferred via the Internet by the store and forward system. The path which your mail message takes to the recipient's mailbox is as follows:

1. You write your message.

2. You connect to the Internet and send your message to your Internet service provider's main server.

3. The message will be temporarily stored on the ISP's server while it checks its address book to ensure that the delivery address is correct.

4. If the server cannot find the address, the message is returned to you.

5. If the server locates the address, it will establish the quickest route across the world to find the destination computer.

6. Your message is then transferred through perhaps a series of servers until it reaches its destination.

7. Upon arrival at the correct server, that server identifies the recipient's name and stores the message in their post box.

8. The recipient will not know they have received a new mail message until they next connect to their local ISP server. Once they do, they will be notified of the new message and can read your e-mail.

Our enthusiasm for using e-mail should, however, be balanced by an awareness of the hidden dangers.

Where do the principle risks lie in the use of electronic mail?

There are a number of areas of risk which we shall consider. In some instances, we will identify these areas but their review in the specific context of e-mail should not be treated as a conclusive study of those issues. It will be seen that the consideration of e-mail dangers is directly referable to other Internet legal exposures. It is essential that you understand those wider risks covered in this work when studying this section.

6.2 COPYRIGHT

Copyright is an intellectual property right which arises automatically (see section 7.2). It affords the authors of literary, dramatic, musical or artistic works the ability to prevent unauthorised copying or exploitation of their work. The law of copyright will protect your copyright on the Internet, just as it will protect your works on other media. An example of how your organisation can protect its copyright by the use of online terms and conditions is given on p. 59.

If someone downloads copyright protected material from the Internet and stores it in whatever form this may constitute a breach of copyright. If a copy of that material is then included in an e-mail message to a third party that may involve multiple breaches of copyright in the work.

How should we proceed when sending an e-mail which we suspect contains copyrighted material?

If copyright material is to be attached to an e-mail, you should ensure that you or your company owns the copyright. Alternatively, if the copyright is owned by another, you should check you are permitted to use it in this way with the owner. In any event, you should consider the inclusion of an appropriate copyright warning notice on the material.

6.3 DEFAMATION

What is defamation?

The most widely accepted definition of 'defamation' is the one formulated by Professor Winfield who said:

Defamation is the publication of a statement which tends to lower a person in the estimation of right thinking members of society generally; or which tends to make them shun or avoid that person.

Only a false statement can amount to defamation. The word 'statement' in the definition has an extended meaning and includes words, visual images, gestures and other methods of signifying meaning.

Defamation takes two forms, libel and slander. The differences between them are that libel is a defamatory statement published in a permanent form, while slander is a defamatory statement published in a transient form.

Another difference between libel and slander is that libel is actionable *per se* (without proof of actual damage) but slander is actionable only on proof of actual damage except in certain specified cases.

The following types of publication are classified as libel.

- writing;
- printing and pictures.

Will Internet communications amount to libel?

While there is no definitive ruling on whether electronically disseminated communications amount to libel, there are good reasons for thinking that in general they will do so.

If you post an article, send an e-mail or create a web page you are committing content to a database on a host computer. The electronic data resides on that database until deleted. This is true whether the data is text, graphics, audio or video. Such information is clearly more than a transient form and is likely to be held to be libel not slander.

The most significant development in this country has been the enactment of the Defamation Act 1996. This Act includes provisions designed to address the question of who is liable and to what standard for defamatory statements disseminated over computer and telecommunications networks such as the Internet.

Defamation liability was one of the first areas of law to come before the courts in the field of online services.

Why has defamation been the most prolific basis of legal actions relating to the Internet to date?

A combination of factors makes this so: the obvious informality of e-mail and the relatively uninhibited discussion which is conducted by Internet news groups. In addition, the cross-border nature of the Internet further heightens the chances of litigation as publication is potentially to the whole world which could affect the level of damages, and the plaintiff could have a wide choice of jurisdictions in which to pursue a defendant.

Before the Defamation Act 1996, English law cast a wide net of liability for publication of a defamatory statement. Anyone who participated in or authorised the publication was liable. So in hard-copy publishing the author, the editor, the publisher, the printer, the distributor and the vendor were all potentially liable. The Internet presents particular difficulties with the distinction between primary publisher and subordinate disseminator. In many cases, it is not possible to distinguish between publication and distribution.

Give me an example of this difficulty.

Online discussion forums or newsgroups allow anyone to place messages directly onto a database accessible by all if they have the appropriate software. The discussion forum proprietor may choose whether or not to exercise the remaining function on selecting content.

However, newsgroups, while usually informal, are not the only form of online publishing. Some publishing on the Internet is more like hard-copy publishing and advertising. It is carefully crafted and vetted and is based on permanent websites or electronic versions of well-known journals and magazines.

It is useful to consider some examples of online dissemination of content.

- An Internet service provider (ISP) provides both Internet access and free web hosting facilities to its customers.

- The owner of a web journal may include a 'letter to the editor' feature on the journal's website. In contrast to the print version, in which letters to the editor are selected and edited for periodic publication, online readers are free to post 'letters' directly to a forum on the website. Other readers can reply in like manner.

- A telecommunications operator agrees to provide and manage a virtual network to enable a group of companies to operate an intranet. All the group's e-mail traffic and requests for documents flow over the network.

- Your web design company receives text from you, its customer, codes the text using HTML (see Chapter 2) and Java and passes the finished product by e-mail to another company which will host your website.

In some of the above examples, the collation function of the original publisher or content provider remains. In other examples, no collation takes place at all, for instance in the case of e-mail traffic.

6.4 THE E-MAIL PROTOCOL

The use of e-mail is now an established feature of modern commercial life. As stated, the principle attraction is cost, speed and ease of communication. As a manager, you must be aware that e-mails are an informal form of communication much like a telephone conversation but in writing. Your organisation should adopt an e-mail protocol as policy which your employees must be made aware of.

What are some of the questions we ought to consider before drawing up an e-mail protocol?

There are a number of questions to address. These include the following:

Who is entitled to send e-mail and to whom?

It is important that your organisation controls who may send and receive e-mails. Clearly, many companies employ several employees in varying capacities. It may be that only certain members of staff need to routinely correspond by use of e-mail, typically senior managers, members of your administration team and personal assistants to directors and partners. The restriction as to who may use the medium will introduce an immediate safeguard against misuse. However, one might wish to specify individuals or organisations which those authorised employees can send e-mails to. Such organisations might only be key suppliers or customers or third parties with whom regular contact is necessary.

Do you have any requirements as to style?

Your organisation may have adopted a standard or pro forma style of communication which should not be departed from. If this is the case then you should ensure e-mail communications are similarly drawn.

Is an e-mail 'business correspondence'?

You should consider whether e-mails to friends and family are acceptable. Your company might consider restricting e-mail messages transmitted or received by employees to essential business communications only.

What issues are relevant to the preparation of an e-mail protocol?

Confidentiality

It should be appreciated that electronic mail is not inherently any more a secure medium of communication than traditional means, even where encryption (see section 5.3) or other security methods are adopted. It may still be possible for persons other than the sender or the intended recipient to gain access to the message at either end. It is therefore important that users of electronic mail consider carefully, before each message is sent, whether electronic mail is the most appropriate means of communication.

Electronic mail must not be sent to a client or customer's business without the express authority of your client or customer. That authority may be given generally or specifically for particular types of communication. At the time any such authority is given, it is the duty of your employee to ensure as far as reasonably possible, that your customer understands and accepts the potential risks of electronic mail, especially if it is proposed to communicate without added security.

In certain circumstances, the contents of an electronic message may contain material which is confidential to a third party. An example would be the forwarding to your customer or client of a confidential message sent to your organisation by a third party. In such cases, it may be necessary to seek permission from the third party before the message is sent.

Copyright

Care must be taken to ensure that electronic communications do not infringe copyright in any works transmitted. This is unlikely to be a problem where the work has been created by your organisation or your customer or client. In the latter case, your customer must consent to the transmission. However, the transmission of material accessed over the Internet, or the retransmission of material received from third parties, may in some circumstances infringe copyright.

Security

Where confidential material is to be sent over the Internet, it is good practice where possible to employ additional means of security. Your customers or clients should always be offered the option of secure means of communication where this is feasible. Where the use of any such means has been agreed with your customer, it is essential that such use takes place on each occasion when an electronic message is sent unless your customer instructs otherwise.

Use of macros

In order to comply with the requirements of legislation, it is essential that all electronic communications on customer matters or confidential electronic communications and all electronic communications which perform the business of correspondence should be composed using a designated macro.

Software and your organisation's systems

No software may be used on your organisation's systems unless it has been approved by, for example, your head of IT. Particular care should be taken to ensure that messages received from third parties do not contain executable files or other software which may have an adverse effect on the operation of those systems.

Records

Your customer or client files must at all times be maintained in accordance with any standards your organisation works to. This might include requirements under ISO 9000 or other industry management standards. Consider whether paper copies of all electronic messages sent and received should be maintained on the relevant customer files so that the file contains a complete record of all communications made. An alternative to the retention of paper records is as follows. Your organisation should ensure that all electronic messages sent and received in relation to customer files are first stored in separate and identifiable folders. These folders should only be accessible to those employees who may need to work on the file in question. The folders should subsequently be stored on disk and kept on the file with a security copy kept in a folder on your organisation's network.

Inappropriate use and content

Electronic messages sent by means of your organisation's systems must properly relate to the business of your company. They should not be used for personal correspondence or for frivolous communications. Excessive use of electronic mail – for example sending an unnecessary quantity of messages to one person or sending messages to an unnecessary number of people – may be grounds for disciplinary proceedings. Your company should make it clear in your e-mail protocol that the possession or distribution of materials in electronic form which is violent, pornographic or otherwise obscene or the use of electronic mail to harass or intimidate other members of staff will usually be grounds for instant dismissal.

Defamation

Particular care should be taken to ensure that electronic messages, whether sent internally or externally, do not contain criticisms of individuals, firms or companies which could be interpreted as libellous (see section 6.3).

Data protection

The holding, processing and disclosure of personal data in electronic form is regulated by the provision of data protection legislation (see Chapter 9). Personal information relating to a living individual who can be identified from that information should not be sent by electronic means unless proper checks have been made to ensure that this will not involve any breach of that legislation.

CHECKLIST: HOW TO MANAGE YOUR COMPANY'S E-MAIL RISKS

- Do you know why e-mail presents certain legal risks?
- Are you familiar with the principles of defamation and why e-mail presents a danger?
- Does your company have an e-mail protocol?
- Do you know the typical provisions found in an e-mail protocol?

7

How to protect your intellectual property over the Internet

7.1 INTRODUCTION

Intellectual property laws are designed to govern creative endeavour in the form of writing, music, drama, art and craft inventions and knowledge. The law enables authors in these mediums to secure proper commercial recognition for their efforts. The Internet enables that creativity, however it manifests itself, to be reduced to bits of information stored electronically and routed around networks.

Digital technology provides new possibilities for copying and distribution. Digital copies are of identical quality to the original and are cheap to produce. The Internet enables rapid mass distribution from anywhere in the world. Copyright will protect works on the Internet, just as it will protect works on other media. Nonetheless, electronic commerce poses fresh problems for the law of intellectual property in general and copyright in particular. In this chapter, we will consider the areas of intellectual property law most relevant to the Internet.

What is the relevance of 'digitisation' to intellectual property as it applies to the Internet?

It is relatively easy to grasp the concept of copyright. However, to understand why the Internet presents particular difficulties to the rights, it is helpful to explain the significance of digitisation.

Digitisation of information is perhaps the most dramatic aspect of the computer revolution. Hitherto, your business communications have been transmitted by graphic means such as letters or designs, or by waves such as soundwaves or electromagnetic signals. However, computers only operate on binary numbers. Thus, information must be reduced to this digital form if it is to be assimilated by a computer. Examples of the advent of digitisation include the CD replacing the LP record. Telephone conversations are increasingly transmitted digitally. If information is capable of conversion 'bits' then it is also capable of transmission over computer networks – the Internet.

What are the advantages of digitisation?

The advantages are twofold. First, copying and transmission can occur without degradation – thus ensuring perfect copies. Second, these copies can be made very quickly and inexpensively.

Your company can send information via the Internet to potentially millions of customers or clients for relatively low transmission costs. Digitisation has caused the cost of copying to fall to virtually zero.

However, with the undoubted improvements to everyday commercial life comes corresponding risk. Information in digital form is much more easily manipulated and adapted than traditional forms of information, and the changes much harder to trace. For your organisation digitisation therefore represents at once unparalleled opportunity and new levels of danger in the form of unlawful copying of your commercial data.

7.2 PATENTS AND THE INTERNET

Explain the basis of patents.

In the UK patents are governed by the Patents Act 1977 and the European Patent Convention. Patents protect novel inventions in the European Union for 20 years from first application. They include software where there is a technical result. Patents protect ideas provided that they are innovative and industrially applicable. With reference to the Internet, patents apply to those unseen but vital technical aspects which make the Internet and the traffic on it possible. These 'unseen aspects' include hardware, software and communications interfaces and protocols which, for example, provide improved and easy access to the Internet. Patents protect the products your organisation may sell on line and also the software you use to enhance the technical capabilities of your website. During the patent life span of 20 years the owner can sell the patented product and prevent anyone else infringing the patent. The owner can also sell or license the patent rights.

How can my company's patents be challenged?

There are three grounds to invalidate your patent:

- lack of novelty;
- lack of inventive step or obviousness;
- insufficiency.

Application for a patent must be made to the UK Patent Office in Newport. However, the mere grant of a patent by that office does not mean that it is valid. Validity is examined afresh by the court. The court will be influenced by the infringement you may allege. Thus, if your patent is construed too widely to catch the infringer it may become invalid. Conversely, if your patent is construed too narrowly to preserve its validity, then there may be no infringement. Your patent will fail for lack of novelty if there is identity between an earlier prior art and your later patent. The test for obviousness or lack of inventive step is whether the uninventive man or team skilled in the art would have made the invention based on the nearest notional starting point. Insufficiency means that the directions in your patent are not sufficient if followed by an ordinary uninventive man not skilled in the art to obtain the result claimed in your patent.

Is software patentable?

In 1996 in a case concerning Fujitsu Limited's patent application no. 9204959.2 the court reviewed a series of earlier cases on this question. In the light of the decision in this case, it is clear that for example, computer programs sitting on the hard disk of a computer are not patentable. The issue is whether when the computer program is run it causes the computer to operate in a novel way and/or produce a novel result.

Why is the risk of infringing patent heightened when trading on the Internet?

As mentioned earlier, different legal jurisdictions give varying treatment to intellectual property rights. While European and UK patent offices may hold certain patents invalid the United States Patent Office appears to be more flexible. More software related patents are granted in the United States. Since, trading on the Internet cannot fail to offer access in the US, your company should be wary. It may be worth investigating obtaining patent protection in the US even if it is not available elsewhere. Moreover, if you are considering copying the techniques of others on the Internet, checking the existence of patent protection in nowhere else other than in the US should be considered.

How can we check to see if our products sold online or an Internet software program we have developed to facilitate our e-commerce strategy is already patented?

Under UK law all patents are registered. This is true of other jurisdictions. The register assists you as an enquirer. It includes the name, address and title of the patent and details of any licences granted. All patents are classified by their subject matter. Searches are computerised and some patents are published on the Internet. IBM runs such a site. Most search engines will list all foreign equivalent patents from a single source. Thus, your company can check to see what patents are in force covering a specific subject matter.

7.3 COPYRIGHT

What is copyright?

Copyright also affects computer programs and broadcasts. The right holders concerned not only include authors but producers, broadcasters and performers. The problem with copyright as it applies to the Internet is that it was developed to deal with the analogue world. The present system of copyright grew out of attempts to control the previous revolution of printing. The Copyright Act 1709 gave an author the exclusive right to print a book. The exclusive rights and the types of work protected have gradually increased through a series of statutes, each reflecting the impact of new technology – radio, film, television. That statutory control culminated in the present legislation, the Copyright, Designs and Patents Act 1988.

What does the 1988 Act protect?

- Literary works (which includes computer programs) and dramatic, musical or artistic works.
- Sound recordings, films, broadcast or cable programmes.
- The typographical arrangement of a published edition.

To be capable of protection, the work must be original. While the 1988 Act does not define 'originality' it is settled case law that the work is not copied and has a minimal amount of creativity. Copyright only comes into existence when the work is recorded, in writing or otherwise.

What does 'writing' include?

Any form of notation or code, whether by hand or otherwise, and regardless of the method by which, or medium in or on which, it is recorded. The contents of a computer screen will be copyrightable – subject to other criteria such as originality.

7.4 TRADE MARKS

Yours organisation's website might be likened to a combination of a shop window and an advertisement hoarding. Your branding has clear import in connection with the Internet and thus the question of trade marks is highly significant. This is because there may not be much opportunity to provide much detail about your product for sale and your brand may of itself provide a good deal of information. Your brand may well be thought of as a badge of origin and quality.

What is a trade mark?

Trade marks distinguish goods and services from one company from those of another. In addition, they serve to protect one's investment in building up goodwill in the name. Trade marks may be registered or unregistered, although both forms are national by nature. Your company's trade marks constitute a form of property which is capable of assignment. Such property may also be charged or licensed to another. It is useful to consider this form of intellectual property in outline while relating its application to the World Wide Web.

7.4.1 Registered trade marks

The laws relating to registered trade marks are far more uniform across the world and thus registered rights are likely to be of most interest to the global trading which the Internet makes possible.

What are the characteristics of a registered trade mark?

One can register a trade mark over one's goods and services if it is capable of being distinguished. The trade mark (sign) can include a word, design or a mix of each. It may also include a distinctive shape or tune. When a trade mark is registered it is designated as covering certain goods or services only. Registration will give your organisation as owner the exclusive right to use that trade mark in the countries in which it is registered.

How can a registered trade mark be infringed?

If anyone uses your registered mark without your authority or licence then such action will amount to an infringement of your mark. Infringement affords you the right to seek an injunction preventing continuing use and an award of damages to compensate you for losses sustained.

How are registered trade marks sought?

In some countries, such as the UK, it is the first person to use a trade mark in relation to the relevant goods or services who has priority right to claim ownership of the mark (i.e. first to use). This is so even though the application for registration takes place many years after its first use. In other countries, it is the first person to register the mark who receives such priority. Unfortunately, ownership of registered trade marks is fragmented around the world. It is not uncommon for trade marks to be in multiple ownership in different countries. It is unusual for any single company to have trade marks in all countries of the world. If therefore an advertisement is placed on the Internet for one company by the trade mark owner in that country it may well infringe the registered trade mark of another company in a country in which the advertisement is accessed and read.

It is only very large companies which will have the financial means to register their brands as trade marks throughout the world. It is likely that your organisation will need to consider the extent of coverage that it requires and what type of infringement risk is acceptable.

How might we deal with such a risk?

It would be prudent to compile a list of your company's most significant markets for the goods in question. At the same time, consider those countries where infringement is most likely to occur and ensure that trade mark registration has at least been sought in those countries.

Why does the Internet provide potential for wider use of trade marks?

The interactive and visual nature of the World Wide Web has resulted in a wider variety of types of trade mark. Examples include a distinctive advertisement, tune or video sequence which turn and morph a graphic from one shape to another. Even single colours can be registered as trade marks provided they have become distinctive of particular goods or services.

How should we depict our trade marks on the Internet?

Be careful not to display your mark in such a way which diminishes its distinctiveness. Thus consistency of colour and style is vital. Moreover, trade mark notices are of equal importance on the Internet as with more traditional mediums. Your company should assert its ownership by stating it owns the mark. It should also make it clear that copying and use may only be done under licence from your company.

My company is considering sponsoring another organisation's web pages. What should we consider?

First, you should ensure a hypertext link is in place to your own website. In these circumstances, the way in which your brand is used is entirely in the hands of the party you are sponsoring. Therefore you should enter into a contract to confirm that such use is proper and also to make clear liability issues.

Why does the global domain name system cause problems with trade marks?

The commercialisation of the Internet has created a new marketplace, a market within which companies wish to exploit their trade marks. The problem is that shared interests in the same or similar trade marks may peacefully coexist in actual reality but not in the virtual marketplace. Where it is quite possible for two separate companies to use the trade mark 'Smith' for different goods, there is only one domain name 'Smith.com'.

There are two difficulties for additional trade mark law in relation to the Internet. First, trade marks are limited in their scope by both specificity and domesticity. The Internet does not respect national boundaries and, currently, has no capacity for differentiation of 'commercial' domain names. Traditional trade mark registers differentiate trade marks on the basis of the goods and/or services with which they are linked. However, all commercial entities, in the eyes of the Internet, are homogeneous. This creates a clash of cultures. Some companies may lose their cyberspace trade mark to another company. The shared rights are many and can only be achieved by one.

CHECKLIST: INTELLECTUAL PROPERTY AND THE INTERNET – COPYRIGHT

- If you download copyright protected material from the Internet and store it, this may constitute a breach of copyright. Similarly, if a copy of such material is included in an e-mail message to a third party, this may involve multiple breaches of copyright in the work.

- If copyright material is to be attached to an e-mail, ensure that your organisation either owns the copyright or that you are permitted to use it in this way by the owner. Additionally, an appropriate copyright warning notice should be put on the material. Copyright arises automatically, but even so it is worth alerting other people to your rights.

- Do you understand the basis of patents?

- Do you know how your company's trade marks will be treated on the Internet?

Advertising and the Internet

8.1 BACKGROUND

In the introduction to this work it was suggested that business had not exclusively driven the development of the Internet to date. The position is undoubtedly changing and the next phase of online evolution is fuelled by the ready appreciation of its commercial application. Nonetheless in this country and elsewhere businesses have been quicker to realise the advertising and marketing potential of the Internet than they have in recognising its potential as a worldwide trading medium. The advertising and promotional component of the Internet may well far exceed the transactional. In this chapter we will examine the legal issues which relate to advertising on the Internet.

The state of advertising on the Internet at present is not dissimilar to that of television advertising in the early 1950s – using models from older media while developing methods precisely suited to the new medium. Advertising on the Internet is likely to continue to evolve.

What are some of the known commercial factors in relation to Internet advertising?

Your company's advertising will be interactive and based on a model in which your customer comes to you. Until the advent of the Internet, interactive advertising or marketing activity had been conducted face to face. The World Wide Web enables your company to engage its prospects in the advertising itself. A major challenge to advertisers over the next decade will be finding ways to fully utilise this capability. Involving your online customer in your advertising message can build long-term customer commitment.

The most common form of Internet advertising is 'banner advertising'. Banner adverts are no longer just static files but may include animation, direct response and other interactivity. Web advertising is fairly simple in concept. The company decides it wants to place a banner advertisement on a website and negotiates with the owner of the website. Usually, advertising rates are set based on a certain cost per thousand impressions (CPM). These impressions are measured by the owner of the website based on the number of times the banner is seen by visitors. At the end of the period, the website owner invoices the advertiser. It is calculated by multiplying the CPM by the number of impressions during that period.

How is my organisation's website accessed?

An online customer will enter your company's domain name into their web browser. The web browser looks this up and then contacts the Internet server and asks for the correct web page. Finally, the file that contains the web page is sent back over the Internet, decoded and displayed correctly by the browser.

What form might my company's online advertising take?

The opportunities for your business to advertise online include advertising in online publications and banner advertising. The legal issues that affect your corporate advertising in the traditional media have equal application to your Internet advertising strategy.

Before considering online advertising, it is well to briefly set out the legal background to advertising production in the UK. In this country, advertising is regulated by voluntary codes. There are, however, many statutes which affect advertising. For example, there are some offences relating to misleading advertising. In addition, certain sectors such as alcohol, cigarettes and financial product advertisements are subject to more stringent regulation. The principal voluntary code in the UK is the British Codes of Advertising Practice (The Codes). They are drawn up by the Committee of Advertising Practice.

Who monitors compliance with the codes?

The Advertising Standard Authority (ASA) is charged with this duty. The ASA is independent.

The Codes set out the rules for what is acceptable in advertisements, direct marketing and sales promotions. The Codes cover all non-broadcast media advertising. Broadcast commercials fall within the responsibility of the Radio Authority and the Independent Television Committee.

There is a much stricter regime relating to advertising regulations than in the general law. Your company's advertisement claims require a level of justification in excess of that necessary for its editorial.

What penalties arise if my company's online advertisement breaks the Codes' rules?

The ASA will ask your company to withdraw or amend its advertisement. Other sanctions include adverse publicity, the refusal of further space, removal of trade incentives and finally legal proceedings. These are by referrals from the ASA to the Office of Fair Trading (OFT) under the Control of Misleading Advertisements Regulations 1988 (CMAR). The OFT can obtain an injunction against your company to prevent it from repeating the same or similar claims in future advertisements.

The first problem which Internet advertising highlights is the proper application of advertising standards in the right circumstances. The distinction between advertising material and editorial on a website can become blurred. This is exasperated by the seamless linking (see section 2.6) of pages on the web which renders it difficult to separate the two. This difficulty may lead to the inadvertent extension of advertising content restrictions to editorial contents. At the time of writing, there is no reported case concerning how an English court would approach the question. However, the issue was considered in the Irish case of *Dunnes Stores Limited* v. *Mandate*.[1]

The case was founded on the Irish equivalent to the UK Control of Misleading Advertising Regulations 1988. A trade union representing a plaintiff's workforce placed an advertisement in the national press seeking to justify strike action by the union's members over Christmas pay. The Irish Supreme Court held that the trade union's advertisement had nothing to do with the promotion of the supply of goods or services and so was not 'advertising'.

When considering advertising and the Internet, the most vexing issue is jurisdiction. The difficulty in properly regulating electronic commerce advertising is trying to apply national frameworks of laws and regulations to adverts disseminated to the world at large. An online advertisement is, in theory, subject to the laws of every country in which it is accessed by an Internet user. Thus far the ASA have focused on websites which originate in the UK. If it is faced with a foreign website, it may be able to refer the complaint to an equivalent regulatory body in the foreign jurisdiction. The breach of non-domestic regulations as a result of the global 'reach' of the Internet was illustrated in *United States* v. *Thomas*,[2] a US court case. In that case, the operators of a pornographic electronic bulletin board in California were convicted of criminal obscenity laws by a federal court in Tennessee. The conviction was founded on Tennessee standards of decency.

Is the question of whose law applies to online advertisement regulation settled?

No. At present there is no international unanimity on the issue. The approach which seems to be adopted is that the laws of the country of 'publication' will apply, that is the country in which there is evidence of 'directed' activity. This is illustrated by an incident involving the English registered Virgin Atlantic Airways. In 1996 Virgin was fined by the US Department of Transportation for a misleading advertisement on its UK server. The inaccuracy related to the quoting of erroneous fares and listing a fare that was no longer available on flights from the USA.

What will be treated as 'directed' activity?

The simple inclusion of information on your organisation's website will not, of itself, be conclusive evidence of directed activity, if there is something about the information making it clear it is targeted at customers in a particular country.

Can we include a disclaimer in our corporate website making the position clear?

The language of your advertisement may be relevant to an extent. A disclaimer may help to clarify who is included in the target audience. An example might be 'this offer is only available for consumers in France'. Such a disclaimer will, however, be construed narrowly and have no legal effect in some countries.

What other safeguards should my company pursue when launching our online advertisement strategy?

While it will be impractical for you to obtain legal clearance in every jurisdiction throughout the world, there are some general principles to adopt. In order to minimise the risk of infringing the advertising regulations of other countries you should take the following steps. Obtain legal and trade mark clearance in your target countries and in countries in which your electronic business has a presence or assets. On a purely practical level, you might consider how costly it might be to change your online advertisement if it were challenged. Would a competitor in fact be able to prove actual damage? Finally, it may well be that the authorities in a given country will take a 'laissez-faire' approach to your Internet advertisement.

My company engages the services of an advertising agency. What issues should we consider?

The issue of your Internet advertising strategy must be discussed fully with your agency. The risk that your business could incur liability for breach of foreign advertising regulations makes it essential for the contract with your agency to lay down clear lines of responsibility for ensuring legal compliance of advertising materials.

8.2 YOUR WEBVERTISING AGREEMENT

A significant development of the commercialisation of the Internet has been the commercial sponsorship of websites.

Website marketing and advertising is highly important to a successful e-commerce strategy. One only has to reflect on the plethora of television advertisements which promote corporate and retail websites. Usually such promotion is part of a wider advertising campaign. Your organisation may wish to sell to others rights to advertise on your website. This advertising can be in the form of banner adverts, hyperlinks and browser windows which start up automatically. You may wish to distinguish between a 'sponsor', who is entitled to a more prominent place on your site, and other advertisers who will receive lesser billing. From the point of view of the advertiser, it will want to be clear not only about the rights it receives in isolation but also its position within the hierarchy of rights.

What issues should we consider if we allow others to advertise on our website?

Proper payment for the space and removing liability for displaying the advert, because trade mark or copyright infringements are primary concerns. If entering into an arrangement with another company to enable them to advertise on your site, your webvertising agreement should cover the following:

- *The rights being granted in respect of your website.* These should be determined. Is your advertiser to have exclusive rights? Are there categories of advertising within which the advertiser will have exclusivity, e.g. that it will be the only food retailer on your site?

- *Payment structure and triggers.* You should consider whether payment will be calculated on a base fee, or per display or click through, or upon ultimate sale.

- Your *responsibilities* and those of your advertiser in relation to appropriateness of adverts should be clearly understood.

- *Licences.* It would be prudent to enter into a limited licence for the use of graphics and/or text and trade marks used in the advertisements.

- *Indemnities.* You should consider inclusion of indemnities to limiting your liability.

- *Termination.* Termination of the webvertising agreement should be clear. In addition, the agreement should set out what will happen upon termination. Usually, materials should be destroyed and web pages changed. If the agreement is terminated rapidly, all payments due under the same should become immediately due and payable.

- *Nature of relationship.* The agreement will only be for advertising cooperation. It should state clearly that it does not create an agency or joint venture between your company and your advertisers.

- *Positioning and size.* Your advertiser will wish to specify where on the website its advertisement will appear. The form and size of the advert relative to other text and other graphics should be clear. With paper-based advertising campaigns sizes are constant. However, Internet advertising involves a consideration of the working of HTML (see section 2.1) and the operation of the web browsers which will be used to access the site. Your advertiser may wish to set up the technical details of how, in particular, its logo is created so as to ensure that it both downloads at an acceptable speed and is attractive.

- *Updating.* Some advertisers may want some contractual assurance that your web page itself will be changed over time to keep up with new versions or releases of relevant browsers, or, conversely, that it will remain usable with older versions.

- *Website promotion obligations.* If your site relates to a campaign by your company in other media, advertisers may wish to have assurances about the promotion of your site within that campaign, such as the inclusion of your website URL (uniform resource locator) on posters and other forms of advertising. Conversely, and particularly where there is one major sponsor, your company might wish to oblige that sponsor to promote your site as part of the sponsor's own advertising.

■ *Hypertext links.* Both your company and your advertiser will have concerns relating to the hypertext links from the advertisement to your advertiser's own web page. Your advertiser will want to make sure that the link is correctly created and that your company is obliged to update it correctly if there is a change in the URL of your advertiser's website. Your advertiser may also wish to ensure that the link can be triggered either from the text message or a graphic. You should ensure that the link to your advertiser's website will not give rise to any liability to third parties for defamation (see section 6.3).

■ *Intellectual property.* Your advertiser will wish to specify the extent of the right of your company to use any trade or service marks on your site and to ensure that you apply the marks consistently with any standard guidelines. The form of the advertising in general may concern your advertiser and they will wish to have prior approval of relevant copy.

You should seek an indemnity in respect of third-party claims arising from use of your advertiser's marks on the Internet.

■ *Information about visitors to your site.* It will be of interest to your advertiser and your company who visits your site. This is because you will need to justify your advertising rate card. Your advertiser will need to judge whether their site is an appropriate place to advertise.

CHECKLIST: ADVERTISING AND THE INTERNET

■ Has your company considered the merits of allowing advertising on its website?
■ Do you know how advertising is regulated on the Internet?
■ Has your company prepared a comprehensive webvertising agreement?

NOTES

1. *Dunnes Stores Limited* v. *Mandate* (1996) FED Ap 0032 (6 CIR) (ii C2).
2. *United States* v. *Thomas* (1996) 2 CMLR 120.

Data protection and the Internet

The Internet's greatest attraction is that it is essentially an open environment. It exists to publicise information and the sheer wealth and diversity of its content encourages browsing. However, the maintenance of privacy is key to the development of the World Wide Web. The protection of data transmitted electronically is subject to a framework of regulation which has application to more traditional mediums. In this section, we shall examine the legal protection which prevails in the UK and how your organisation can achieve compliance.

9.1 BACKGROUND

Concern over the information-gathering ability of computers and the invasion of citizens' rights has been manifest for over 40 years. The unlawful processing of personal data represents a violation of fundamental human rights and is treated as such in most countries. The information superhighway collects, processes and transfers prodigious amount of personal data. Your online customer will of necessity have to disclose their home address, contact details, credit card number and other personal details if purchasing from your website. Unless they have absolute confidence your organisation will keep that data secure, it will not be volunteered and your e-commerce strategy will fail. Thus your organisation has an obligation to trade responsibly. It is important to appreciate that company directors are personally liable for the accuracy of their databases and individuals can sue not just for financial losses directly resulting from inaccurate or wrongly disclosed data, but for any breach of the law and for any resultant distress.

9.2 THE DATA PROTECTION ACT 1998

What is the current regulatory position in this country?

The law governing processing of personal data is embodied in the Data Protection Act 1998. However, it is important to note that this legislation is part of a unification of legal treatment of the issue within the EU.

In 1995 the European Parliament and Council issued the EU Directive on Data Protection (96/46/EEC). The Directive covers the protection of individuals with regard to the processing of personal data and the free movement of such data. It is that Directive that led to the introduction of the Data Protection Act 1998. The Act has been in force since March 2000 and replaced the Data Protection Act 1984. The 1998 Act is more extensive than the 1984 Act, and while the Act sets out the overall legal framework, much of the detail will be contained in secondary legislation.

What are the most significant additions to the regulation which the Act introduces?

One major difference is the new definition of 'processing':

> *obtaining, recording or holding the information or data or carrying out any operation or set of operations on the information or data.*

For many organisations, especially those that are heavily reliant on IT to run their business processes, the new Act involves an extensive compliance programme.

In what circumstances is the 1998 Act applied?

First, if you are 'established' in the UK, that is if you are ordinarily resident, a UK limited company, partnership or unincorporated business, and in addition if you have an office, branch or agency which carries on any activity in this country. Second, if you are not established here but use equipment in this country for processing data. Finally, if data is exported to you from this country.

Throughout the EU corresponding legislation is in place subject to minor variation. However, it can be seen that, for example, a website hosted in the United States and controlled by a US entity will not be subject to our law. This is so even if it processes information obtained from a customer in this country. Immediate conflict occurs on this issue because the EU Data Protection regime prohibits online customer profiling which is acceptable in the United States. At the time of writing, this problem is being negotiated between the EU and US. Unless it is resolved data transfer to the US could be blocked.

What type of information is covered by the Act?

'Personal data', that is data relating to a living individual who can be identified directly or indirectly. Such people will include your employees, suppliers, customers and business contacts.

What does the Act require my organisation to do?

If your organisation either alone, or with others, determines the purposes for which personal data is processed it will be treated as a 'data controller'. There can be more than one data controller. Your company must:

- notify the Data Protection Commission of its identity. In addition, you have to provide a description of and the purposes for which personal data is to be processed by you. It is clear that all UK-based electronic commerce businesses need to follow the notification procedure. Multinational businesses may need to comply with the notification requirements in several countries;

- process the personal data fairly and comply with the Data Protection Principles;

- provide access to the data which you hold on a person. This is so that that person can check and correct their records and prevent some types of processing. The new system is intended to be a simplified formalistic system. Your organisation must notify the Commissioner of the registrable particulars and pay the prescribed fee.

Explain the basic Data Protection Principles.

The 1998 Act and related EU regulation set out eight principles which your organisation must follow:

1. All personal data which you hold must be processed fairly and lawfully. It must not be processed unless one of the conditions at Schedule 2 is met. More stringent conditions apply to the processing of sensitive personal data. These are set out in Schedule 3 to the 1998 Act. The 1998 Act defines 'sensitive personal data' as 'personal data consisting of information as to a data subject's racial or ethnic origin, political opinions, religious beliefs, or other beliefs of a similar nature, membership of a trade union, physical or mental health or condition, sexual life, or commission or alleged commission or proceedings in relation to any of them'. Processing sensitive data will only be legitimate if the data subject has given his 'explicit consent'. If sensitive personal data is used, at least one condition at Schedule 3 must also be met. It is clear that personal data will not be considered to be processed 'fairly' unless certain information is provided or made readily available to the individual concerned. The information to be given to data subjects must include the identity of the data controller, the purpose or purposes for which the data is intended to be processed 'and any further information which is necessary' having regard to the specific circumstances in which the data is to be processed, to enable processing in respect of the data subject to be fair.

    Where data is obtained directly from the data subject, the requisite information should normally be provided at, or be made available from, the time of data collection.

How does the Internet impinge upon sensitive data?

In the Internet context, some activities may relate overtly to sensitive data. In other cases, the association may be more subtle or uncertain. For example, does the hosting by an online service provider of a discussion or chat forum relating to a particular medical condition or treatment constitute processing of sensitive personal data?

In that case, a relevant question would be whether the data consisted of information as to 'the data subject's physical or mental health or condition'. The answer would depend on the facts. For example, comments posted by the patient about his or her health probably would be sensitive personal data whereas comments posted by a surgeon in relation to a particular surgical procedure without reference to any patient probably would not be sensitive personal data.

How does the requirement to deal with data fairly affect our website?

When information is contained in a form on a website it is immediately capable of being processed as personal data. Notifications of the uses and disclosures of the data should therefore be given at the beginning of the form so that your customer can decide, on the basis of full information, whether or not to proceed with the transaction. In the Internet context, it should be easy to provide the requisite information via an e-mail message or a notice on a web page. For a specimen notice, see p. 62.

2. Personal data shall only be obtained for one or more specified and lawful purpose. It should not be further processed in a manner incompatible with that purpose.

3. Personal data must be adequate, relevant and not excessive in relation to the purpose for which it is processed. While your online enquirer may be willing, in the course of a transaction, to give your organisation a great deal of personal information, your business has a duty to protect them from themselves and their generosity. This has important implications for data collection via the Internet. Many website operators require regular visitors, and in some cases also occasional surfers to register before gaining access. It is very important that your company as a website operator makes clear precisely why non-essential questions are being asked and whether a response is optional. For example, capturing an e-mail address may be necessary for the provision of a particular service, whereas collecting information, for example, about gender, marital status, income and age may be irrelevant or excessive. Such data may of course assist you in building profiles of visitors to your site for your own or third-party marketing purposes. If your declared registered purpose of the processing does not extend to cover processing for that purpose, such processing would probably be unfair. There are now technological solutions to this problem. These are being given strong support by European Data Protection Commissioners.

   In 1995 the Information and Privacy Commission in Ontario, Canada and the Registratiekamer in the Netherlands jointly produced a report entitled *Privacy – Enhancing Technologies: The Path to Anonymity*. The thrust of the report was thus. At present, people are compelled to reveal their identity in a host of circumstances – when using a credit card, subscribing to a magazine, etc. An identifiable record of each transaction is usually created and recorded in a computer database somewhere. The report suggested the use of privacy-enhanced technologies. These can be explained by comparison with a Venetian masked ball. At such events guests arrive and are identified as people whom the host has invited to attend. They wear a mask to hide their identity. They have been authorised to participate in the party but nobody knows who they are. Privacy-enhanced technologies perform the same function in an electronic environment. The user arrives at the system and encounters the 'identity protector'. Once it has established identity it gives the user a mark or 'authorised pseudo identity'. Working through the identity protector the user can enter into binding transactions. However, the user is in control of information regarding their identity being passed onto the system. Any attempts by the system to discover the user's true identity are caught by the identity protector.

Development of these technologies is being funded by the European Commission and is encouraged by all the European Data Protection Commissioners. It is entirely possible that very shortly privacy law and technology will come together to make it illegal in Europe to use e-commerce systems which do not contain identity protectors. Unfortunately, each resolution to a problem often creates a further one. For example, identity protectors must not hinder the investigation of money laundering or tax evasion, terrorism or serious crime.

4. Personal data must be accurate and kept up to date where necessary.

5. Personal data processed for any purpose shall not be kept for longer than is necessary for that purpose.

6. Personal data must be processed in accordance with the rights of data subjects under the Act.

7. Appropriate technical and organisational measures will be taken against unauthorised or unlawful processing of personal data. Such action will also be taken in the case of accidental loss, destruction or damage to personal data. Given the degree of public concern regarding the security, or otherwise, of communications and transactions via the Internet, this principle needs to be considered carefully, notwithstanding that public concerns may be vastly overstated.

If your company uses a data processor such as an Internet service provider or other third party which processes data on your behalf, for example by hosting the website, you will be in breach of this seventh principle unless both of the following criteria are satisfied:

  – The processor provides sufficient guarantees in respect of the technical and organisational security measures governing the processing to be carried out, and you take reasonable steps to ensure compliance with those measures.

  – The processing is governed by a written contract requiring the processor to act only as instructed by the controller and to comply with security obligations equivalent to those imposed on the controller. In the Internet context, you will therefore need to ensure your company has appropriate and properly documented contractual arrangements in place with, *inter alia*, your ISP and website hosters.

8. Personal data must not be transferred to a country or territory outside the EU. The exception is if that country ensures an adequate level of protection for the rights and freedoms of data subjects in relation to the processing of personal data.

   It is this eighth principle that causes most uncertainty about the scope of the 1998 Act in practice. Broadly, the UK Data Protection Registrar advises that, if an adequate level of protection does not exist in the destination country, that is there are no adequate data protection laws in force, your organisation is required to assess whether adequate protection exists for the transfer in question, taking into account all the circumstances.

In the context of the Internet, how might the data protection regime be infringed?

Information may be made accessible by means of the Internet in two alternative ways:

■ by use of the Internet's e-mail facility; and

■ by inclusion in material held on an Internet site such as your organisation's web page.

Access may be limited to a closed user group or it may be unrestricted. Where you transmit information through the Internet or e-mail there is usually only an intentional disclosure to the identified address. However, your e-mail may be carried over networks which pass through countries other than the UK (if this is the country of original transmission) and the country of your addressee. These other countries may not have data protection regimes, and may not provide protection akin to that afforded by the 1998 Act. Thus you may inadvertently breach data protection along the route taken.

What rights do those whose data my organisation processes have?

Data subjects have extensive rights under the Act. As an electronic commerce business, you must comply. A data subject may write to your organisation and ask to be supplied with a description, purposes and disclosures made of or a copy of any personal data being held. Your organisation must respond to that request within 40 days on receipt of a single fee (the fee level is to be set by regulations). A data subject also has the right to prevent processing likely to cause them damage. In addition, an individual has the right to claim compensation if your organisation contravenes certain requirements of the Act. In the case of inaccurate data, an individual can apply to the court for correction, blocking, erasure or destruction.

Individuals must also be notified when data is being collected and be told how it may be used and who is collecting it.

What are the penalties for breaching the Act?

It has always been, and continues to be, a criminal offence not to register where appropriate data is held by your organisation. The penalties are a fine up to £5000 if convicted in a magistrate's court but are higher if convicted in a Crown Court. A larger threat is that of having to pay compensation where damage has been caused by the loss, unauthorised destruction or disclosure of personal data.

What are the problems of applying the data protection rules to the Internet?

The transborder data flow rules in the 1998 Act seem to be based on a presumption that international data traffic always follows precise and predictable routes. This assumption is fundamentally at odds with the way in which information is in fact conveyed via the Internet for at least two reasons.

- First, the Internet, which is a vast and dynamically configured network of networks, has a so called 'self-healing' architecture. Messages or data representing information of any other kind are split into 'pockets' which are sent via the most efficient routing at any given instance. Transfers are thus not predictable in geographical terms.

- Secondly, because Internet e-mail can be downloaded and web pages can be viewed from anywhere on the planet, the sender of the message or operator of a website has no effective control over where a particular message will be downloaded or web page viewed. Consequently, it must be assumed that data contained in Internet e-mail messages and web pages potentially may be transferred to any country in the world, without regard to the adequacy or otherwise of the local data protection safeguards, if any. Moreover, the sheer volume of personal data which is conveyed by the Internet and the vast number of data transfers make it inconceivable that even a significant minority of transfers can be regulated in any meaningful way under the cumbersome rules established by the 1998 Act.

CHECKLIST: THE DATA PROTECTION ACT 1998
AND THE INTERNET

- Do you understand the ambit of the Data Protection Act 1998?
- Are you familiar with the eight Data Protection Principles and their significance to your online presence?
- Is your organisation registered under the Act?

Bibliography

Beck, Walter H. and Senne, Jeff (1996) *Cyber Power for Businesses – How to Profit from the Information Superhighway*. Career Press.

Chissick, Michael and Kelman, Alistair (1999) *Electronic Commerce – Law and Practice*. Sweet & Maxwell.

Cohen, Peter S. (1999) *Net Profit*. Jossey-Bass.

Collin, Simon, *Doing Business on the Internet*. Kogan Page.

Davies, F. R. (1982) *Contract*, 4th edn. Sweet & Maxwell.

DTI (1998) *Building the Knowledge Driven Economy*, White Paper.

DTI (1999) *Promoting Electronic Commerce*, Consultation on Draft Legislation and the Government's Response to the Trade and Industry Committee.

Elliott, Sara (1998/99) 'Meta-tags – what are they?', *Corporate Briefing*, December/January.

Furriston, M. P. (1999) *Law of Contract*, 9th edn. Butterworths.

Flint, David (1998) 'Tag-links and frames – for use of fact?', *Business Law Review*, October.

House of Commons (1999) *Electronic Communications Bill*, as presented to the House of Commons on 18 November, Session 1999–2000.

Jenis, Simon (1997) 'Doing business on the Internet', *PLC*, vol. VIII, no. 2.

Kelleher, Dennis (1998) 'Internet domain name disputes', *New Law Journal*, 29 May.

Lacte, Douglas (1998) 'Trading on the Internet: avoiding the black holes', *Corporate Briefing*, October.

Lownes, Michael (1999) 'Regulating electronic commerce', *Solicitors Journal*, 19 January.

Maddox, Kate and Blantonhorn, Dan (1998) *Web Commerce – Building a Digital Business*. John Wiley & Sons.

Maros, Stephen (1999/2000) 'Electronic signatures: the technical and legal ramifications', *Corporation and Law*, vol. 10, no. 5.

Millard, Christopher (1999) *Data Protection and the Law*. Sweet & Maxwell.

Mocharg, Mary Anne, Marsell, Aaren and Hunter, Gill (1999) 'The message is beware', *Estates Gazette*, 19 June.

Pullan, Tim (1999) 'Data Protection Act 1998 – preparing for compliance', *Computers and Law*, vol. 10, no. 3.

Smith, Graham J. M. (ed.) (1999) *Internet Law and Regulation*, 2nd edn. Sweet & Maxwell.

York, Stephen and Shia, Kenneth (eds) *E-commerce – A Guide to the Law of Electronic Business*. Butterworths.